A Chronological Review of the Past Millennium

By MIKE BROWN

FOREST PUBLISHING

First published in 2000 by FOREST PUBLISHING, Woodstock, Liverton, Newton Abbot, Devon TQ12 6JJ

British Library Cataloguing in Publication Data

A catalogue record for this book is available from the British Library.

ISBN 0–9527297–8–4

Forest Publishing

Editorial, design and layout by:
Mike Lang

Typeset by:
Carnaby Typesetting, Torquay, Devon TQ1 1EG

Printed and bound in Great Britain by:
The Latimer Trend Group, Plymouth, Devon PL6 7PL

Cover photographs:

Front – Vur Tor, rocky sentinel of the northern fen (q.v. 1000).

Back – The view from the flank of Vur Tor, over a wilderness still largely untouched by human hand (q.v. 2000).

Contents

Introductory Notes & Acknowledgements

To mark the turn of a new millennium, I felt that it would be an interesting idea to compile a record of selected episodes from Dartmoor's history since AD 1000, and the entries herein represent the results of that research, which I trust will form a useful addition to the bookshelves of all with an interest in the upland region at the heart of Devon – often dubbed 'the last great wilderness in southern England'.

At the outset it was not my intention to record a great amount of detail about any of the events, so I have purposely kept the comments to a minimum in order to include as many entries as possible. It is my hope that some of these brief notes might fire the imagination of readers, prompting them to seek out for themselves more information on subjects or incidents which particularly arrest their attention, and/or to visit some of the locations mentioned in the text, and if such proves to be the case then the book has successfully accomplished part of what it was intended to achieve. For those with a wider knowledge of Dartmoor's history, the compilation will, hopefully, also serve as a handy source to which reference can be made for the clarification of the years in which various events took place.

I have tried to encompass as wide a range of topics as possible; from events and incidents of major historical importance, the records of various properties at different periods of history and some of the principal families of the region, through to what might be thought of as being quite ordinary and mundane occurrences. All of these happenings, major and minor, of nationwide importance or of purely localised interest, and the actions of all of the participants, whether lords or labourers, saints or sinners, have had their part to play in the history of Dartmoor over the past thousand years.

With such a wealth of historical facts from which to choose during certain periods of history, and in particular years, the entries herein obviously reflect purely personal choices to some extent, although I hope that nothing of major significance has been inadvertently neglected. And I also trust that the coverage of topics is broad enough to satisfy the curiosity of all readers, each with their own widely varying interests.

Conversely, and hardly surprisingly, it has proved very difficult to track down information from the very earliest periods, a problem which is compounded by the fact that most early deeds were not dated at all. Consequently, historians are unable to assign absolute dates to them; they have to be approximated by reference to the persons named in them or known dateable events which are connected with them.

A few entries from particular periods thus, of necessity, touch on the wider aspects of Devonian and/or English history, for references to Dartmoor (or even Devon as a whole) are so few and far between: it is a curious circumstance, for example, that the history of Devon seems to be very poorly documented in the twelfth and fifteenth centuries. I have not hesitated to include these types of entries for, of course, edicts laid down by the Crown and the Church affected the inhabitants of Dartmoor just as much as the rest of the nation, and so are not entirely divorced from the principal subject matter, although events which have no direct relevance to the region have also had to be considered for a couple of dozen or so of the entries for particular years during these early centuries.

However, notwithstanding the paucity of local references and information from certain periods of history, I have, in fact, managed to discover something of note to record against every single year over the past millennium – although, as will be seen from some of the entries, I have occasionally had to resort to rather 'devious' methods in order to achieve such a complete coverage! Nevertheless, these latter types of entries have been devised with the aim of extending the historical period under review – in referring to anniversaries of important events and occurrences etc – and so are not without interest or relevance, and can be considered as a 'bonus'.

A list of all of the wide variety of sources which have been consulted for the compilation of these notes would itself run to a few dozen pages, so there is regrettably no room for one. And, in the absence of a reference list of published and manuscript sources, a general acknowledgement is hereby given to all authors, editors and publishers of all books, learned journals, magazines, newsletters and newspapers, and to the authors of unpublished treatises, research works and manuscripts etc. Their contributions, both great and small, have recorded and preserved parts of Dartmoor's long history for the benefit of future generations of researchers and enquirers, without which no listing of the type provided within these pages could have even been contemplated in the first place, let alone filled with such a varied amount of information.

Similar acknowledgements are also hereby given to all those who have written, compiled, edited and published the major treatises and works on general English and European history, which have also been consulted.

Many thousands of original documents and archive materials held at the City of Plymouth & West Devon Record Office have also been examined during the course of many years of research into Dartmoor-related subjects and families. Original archive materials have been cited in as many instances as possible for the years for which such documentary references have been discovered, most especially from the post-medieval era, the period within which my own research is primarily concentrated.

My particular thanks are due to Paul Brough, Anne Morgan and other members of staff at the City of Plymouth & West Devon Record Office, and to Ann Landers, John Smith (now retired) and other members of staff at the Plymouth Central Library Local Studies & Reference Departments, for their invaluable assistance with my quest for information. And also to all those with whom I have corresponded and spoken to over the years, many of whom have provided data on aspects of Dartmoor's history into which they have conducted their own research, and/or have passed on information about places and families of which they have local knowledge and expertise.

And finally, once again, I reiterate my hope that the range of topics covered, and the extracts which I have selected for inclusion, within these pages is broad enough to satisfy readers with a wide variety of different interests, and will be a source of inspiration which will prompt them to delve further into the long and eventful history of the Dartmoor region – 'the last great wilderness in southern England'.

Mike Brown,

January 1st AD 2000

*****

"Llydanforde, Saxon, of the Noyse of the Water" – which the Danes "pierced" in AD997 (q.v. 1000).

The Eleventh Century

1000 As the rising sun ushers in a brand new millennium, west Devon is still in a state of upheaval. An ancient manuscript records that three years earlier "Llydanforde, Saxon, of the Noyse of the Water, Towne and Castle in Devonshire, standing upon the River Tamar, whereunto an Army of Danes pierced in the time of King Ethelrede, and burned it, spoilinge the People". Tavistock was also sacked by the Vikings, and the great Benedictine abbey "founded in 974", and completed by Ordulf in 981, was razed to the ground. Far away from these scenes of conflict, a lone traveller of the wastes looks out from the summit of Vur Tor, rocky sentinel of the northern fen, to survey the scene and sees...nothing! A vast expanse of untamed moorland stretches before him, totally untouched by human hand, seen by only a few. What will become of this wild place once so-called 'civilisation' gets its hands on it?...

1001 One of the Anglo-Saxon Chronicles records that "This year there was a great commotion in England...Danes...spread terror and devastation...plundering and burning and desolating the country...they came into Devonshire...burned Teignton, and also many other goodly towns that we cannot name".

1002 The Massacre of St Brice's Day – many Danes throughout England are put to death.

1003 A son is born to Aethelred II. Later to become King Edward the Confessor, succeeding to the throne in 1042, his promise to William of Normandy in 1051, and his subsequent death in 1066, would change the course of English history. ◆ Meanwhile, in Devon, the town of Exeter is razed to the ground and the original cathedral reduced to ashes.

1004 England is again subjected to Viking raids and a full scale invasion. ◆ Exeter is betrayed to the Danes by a reeve of Queen Emma.

1005 Aethelred II adopts a policy of appeasing the Viking raiders by bribery.

1006 Richard the Fearless is Duke of Normandy. His great grandson, Richard Fitzgilbert, would marry Rohais, sister of the Walter le Giffard, 3rd Lord of Longueville, who was to fight at the Battle of Hastings. Their grandson, Robert de Tellieres, later assumed the name Giffard, and it is to him that the Giffard family of Devon owe their ultimate ancestry. He also founded the Church of St

Michael's at Brentor (q.v. 1130).

1007 More burning and plundering, mainly in East Anglia and the south coast as far west as Hampshire. £30,000 is given to pay off the Viking raiders.

1008 Is this the year in which (some) Devonians are taxed for the very first time? Aethelred II imposes a tax to raise money in order to build a fleet to fight off continued Danish raids – men possessing 310 hides of land are to provide a galley, and pro rata down to those holding just eight hides, who are to find a helmet and breastplate. His laws also contain an early reference to tithes, decreeing that Plough-Alms to the church are to be paid 15 days before Easter, the Tithe of Young Animals by Pentecost, the Fruits of the Earth by All Saints Day, and Rome-Money by St Peter's Day.

1009 Thurkill invades southern England after the English fleet – "so many of them [ships] as never were in England before" (A-S Chronicles) – is partly destroyed in a storm.

1010 Viking raids continue unabated. ◆ Throughout this period of nationwide upheaval, Lydford continues to mint the coins of the realm – most of the surviving examples of Lydford 'pennies' are now in Scandinavian museums!

1011 Canterbury is plundered by Viking raiders.

1012 Archbishop Aelfeah of Canterbury, captured the previous year, is put to death by the invaders. ◆ A document, dated between 1008 and 1012, probably contains the earliest reference to a Dartmoor placename during the period reviewed here (there are some references to places on Dartmoor which pre-date AD 1000) – it names a place called "aescburnam lande", which has been identified with the site of the modern town of Ashburton.

1013 England comes under Viking rule, and Aethelred II flees to Normandy.

1014 The Saxons of Devon and the rest of southern England reinstate Aethelred II as their king.

1015 The country is divided – Canute ruling the north, Aethelred the south. The latter is succeeded upon his death by Edmund, and further battles for supremacy ensue.

1016 Following the death of Edmund, the whole of England comes under the rule of a Viking king, Canute (or Knut), which at last brings a degree of stability to the united country.

1017 Canute divides England into four regions and appoints himself Governor of Wessex. Brihtric, who had in former years conducted attacks around the southern coasts of Britain, is killed somewhere in Devon.

1018 The tribute demanded by Canute for bringing an enforced peace on the country is £72,000. This vast sum is, apparently, paid, and one must suppose that virtually the entire population (those who possessed land or property), including the men of Devon and Dartmoor, contributed in some way. Canute orders that his reeves should "maintain his people justly...and practice such mercy as seems just" – an early reference to reeves, which suggests that they held much wider powers than they were to enjoy in later times.

1019 Canute spends the winter in Denmark, returning the following year.

1020 One of Canute's laws contains an interesting early reference to the manorial system of heriot payments – "if anyone departs this life intestate...or through sudden death, the lord is then not to take more from his possessions than his legal heriot". A short scale of rates is also provided, a king's thegn being subject to a heriot of four horses, two swords, four spears and as many shields, a helmet, a coat of mail, and 50 mancuses of gold, down to "he who is in a lower position" being subject to a payment of the equivalent of just £2.

1021 Aethalweard, a member of the Old English Royal House, and an earldorman of south west England, is outlawed. ◆ William of Poitiers, who later wrote *Gesta Guillelmi Ducis Normannorum et Regis Anglorum* (Deeds of William, Duke of Normandy and King of England), is born in about this year.

1022 Eadnuth is Bishop of Crediton.

1023 Wulfstan, Archbishop of York, and drafter of the Laws of Canute, dies.

1024 At about this time King Canute's sister is running a white slave trade, selling native English girls to Scandinavia – did any Devonian girls perhaps suffer this fate?

1025 The earliest opportunity during the period under review to celebrate an historical event (as we today celebrate momentous events of the past) – the 200th anniversary of the Battle of Galford, at which the Devonians fought the men of Cornwall.

1026 Some men from Devon (possibly) fight alongside King Canute in Sweden.

1027 Canute reaffirms the tithe dues (q.v. 1008), "which by ancient Law are due to God".

1028 At about this time Walter Giffard is Lord of Longueville. His son, also Walter, will fight on the side of the Conqueror at the Battle of Hastings. (These are the ancestors of the Giffards who, in the 11th century, became settled at Whitchurch, Lamerton and other places on the western edge of Dartmoor.)

1029 The Glunold family, descended from Richard Glunold, grandson of Eystein of Norway, are counts of the Cotentin, the ultimate ancestors of the Devonian family of Daubeney (q.v. 1045). ◆ Of interest to collectors of the curious and absurd, is a record of the first manned flight (!?) in this country – Monk Eilmer, attaching wings to his arms, climbs to the top of Malmsbury Abbey and launches himself into the air; his short vertical 'flight' is summarily interrupted by a sudden impact with the ground, which breaks both of his legs!

1030 Buckfast Abbey is founded by Canute – there appears to be some dispute over this, for some sources state that the abbey was a Saxon one which had been established some two centuries earlier, and perhaps the reference should correctly state that Canute founded a *new* abbey on the site, with a new Order of Monks (q.v. 1276).

1031 King Canute grants $^{1}/_{2}$ hide of land in Mawi (Meavy) to Aetheric.

The Seal of Tavistock Abbey (q.v. 1034).

1032 Robert, Earl of Normandy, dies in Jerusalem and is succeeded by William, later to become King of England. ◆ "The wildfire appeared, such as no man remembered before" (A-S Chronicles).

1033 The bones of St Alphage are transferred from St Paul's to Canterbury Cathedral.

1034 According to a contemporary document, only two monasteries exist west of Dorset, those at Crediton and Tavistock; Buckfast Abbey (q.v. 1030) is not named.

1035 Canute dies and is buried at Winchester.

1036 How truly 'ancient' tithe payments are (q.v. 1008) is not clear, but they would certainly be around for a while yet! In this year men of Devon (and elsewhere) could look forward to paying them on every conceivable type of produce and stock for another eight centuries – until the Tithe Commutation Act of 1836.

1037 Harthacanute, the rightful heir of Canute, is replaced in his absence (he is now living in Denmark) by Harold, who is proclaimed King of all England.

1038 A monk of St Bertin's at St Omer begins writing the *Ecomium* in about this year (it is completed c1040), a three-volume work relating the exploits of King Canute.

1039 A treaty between Norway and Denmark provides Harthacanute with an opportunity to sail for England and claim the throne, but Harold, in fact, dies before he reaches these shores.

1040 Harthacanute becomes king. He reigns for just two years.

1041 At about this time Erdulf holds the manor of Begatore (Bagtor).

1042 The sees of Devon and Cornwall are united under Bishop Lyfing, Abbot of Tavistock. ◆ Edward the Confessor accedes to the throne.

1043 Richard de Glanville establishes himself as Lord of Glanville, near Caen, in France. It is to him that the ancestry of the later Glanvilles of Tavistock can be traced.

1044 The A-S Chronicles record that "this year there was great hunger all over England, and corn so dear as no man remembered".

1045 King Edward gathers a fleet at Sandwich to face the threat of invasion by Magnus of Norway. ◆ William Glunold is banished to Aubigny in Brittany by the Duke of Normandy. (His son, also William, acquired lands in Devon after the Conquest, and, in the 12th century, the family took the name Daubeney, after the place in Brittany to which their ancestor had been banished.)

1046 Lyfing, Bishop of Devon and ex-Abbot of Tavistock, dies. At the moment of his death an earth-shattering crack of thunder is heard across the entire country, feared by many to herald the end of the world.

1047 The A-S Chronicles record that "there was throughout England very much death".

1048 An earthquake occurs in the Midlands.

1049 Raiders from Ireland, harrying the South West, kill Earl Beorn who had been sent in a royal ship, as part of a small fleet, to protect the Devon and Cornish coastal towns.

1050 The levy of Danegeld is abolished which, the A-S Chronicles observe in a gross understatement, "vexed men variously"! ◆ Part of a boundary outlined by the Peadington Charter follows the River Dart up to the Wedeburne (River Webburn), and along this stream as far as Withimoor (Widecombe).

1051 King Edward promises that William, Duke of Normandy, will succeed him as King of England.

1052 The men of Devon, no longer vexed by the taxes (q.v. 1050), find something – or, rather, someone – else against whom to vent their wrath, and rise up against Harold. They are defeated in a series of battles on the Devon/Somerset borders.

1053 Harold, son of Godwine, becomes Earl of Wessex.

1054 Another harsh winter, one of many during this period, inflicts great losses to crops and cattle.

1055 By this year Devon has been divided into 33 hundreds and nearly 400 parishes, the second largest county in England.

1056 Siward of Northumberland, owner of extensive lands on Dartmoor, including the manor of Wifluerde – Warne – in Mary Tavy, and after whom Siward's Cross is said to be named, dies not long after having won (in 1055) a victory in Scotland.

1057 Wakelyn de Ferrariis is Lord of Ferrier in Gastinois, France, father of the Robert de Ferrers who came over with the Conqueror and later established the family in Devon.

1058 Malcolm III becomes King of Scotland, an event which will have a bearing on the future dynasty of the Plantagenet kings of England.

1059 The Reinell family holds the manor of East Ogwell, one of the few ancient Devon gentry families who retained their position after the Conquest. ◆ The 400th anniversary of the founding of the Augustinian monastery at Canterbury.

1060 "There was a great earthquake on the day of the Translation of St Martin" (A-S Chronicles).

1061 A charter of this, or the previous, year, recited in the *Recuil des Actes des Ducs de Normandie,* refers to three Redvers brothers, William, Richard and Baldwin. Owning estates in Reviers, Néhou and Vernon, these are the ancestors of the de Redvers family who were to play such an important role in Devon's medieval history.

1062 Earl Harold invades Wales. ◆ The millennial anniversary of the

Siwards, or Nuns, Cross (q.v. 1056).

defeat, by the Romans, of Queen Boudiccea and the Iceni.

1063 According to Pole, there are less than 350 houses in Exeter at this time. But Polwhele contends that as early as 1222 there were no less than 19 parishes in the city.

1064 The manor of Wodiacome (Widecombe) is held by Edric. But not for very much longer…

1065 The last year of rule for many Anglo-Saxon manorial landowners throughout Dartmoor and across the country as a whole, for the following year the entire nation will come under permanent Viking rule – only these Vikings are three or four generations removed from their Danish ancestors, and like to call themselves Normans...

1066 William of Normandy lands at Pevensey Bay. And the rest, as they say, is history! Sailing with him is Alan Fargent, one of whose followers is Robert Bastardiène, whose descendants would, 548 years later, become lords of the manor of Buckland-in-the-Moor, which title they were to hold for 14 generations, until 1926. Remarkably, the family lineage actually spans a longer period than that covered by this book, for the male Bastardiène line can itself be traced further back, to a 9th century Cornish count – how's that for an extended Dartmoor family tree! The present compiler understands that not even the Courtenays can eclipse this, for it appears that their tree can be traced only to Godfrey, Earl of Ewe, son of Richard, 1st Duke of Normandy, the grandfather of William the Conqueror. One line of the Bastard ancestry goes back even further, through female lines, to Cerdic, who became the self-appointed first king of the West Saxons in AD 495 – this lineage can be followed in an unbroken descent spanning no less than 51 generations!

1067 A Saxon revolt in the West of England is suppressed. Exeter capitulates after a three-week siege.

1068 Many Saxon landowners on Dartmoor are dispossessed, and the peasantry put into service under the new feudal lordships.

1069 North Bovi is one of many Dartmoor manors given to Judhel of Totnes, who installs Turgis as his under-lord there.

1070 Lands in Widecombe are held by Alric, as sub-tenant of Walscin de Donay.

1071 The writing of one of the Anglo-Saxon Chronicles – known as the Parker Chronicle, the oldest of the four Chronicles – using older manuscripts and documents as its sources, may have begun about this time. However, this interpretation of events might be slightly in error, and the Parker Chronicle could possibly have been started very much earlier, but not actually taken to Canterbury

The Manor House Hotel – built in the early 19th century on the probable site of the ancient manor house of North Bovey (q.v. 1069).

until c1071. The earliest of what can be correctly described as a true 'Chronicle' of events was begun by monks during the reign of King Alfred, but whether this is the Parker Chronicle or the latter is a later copy of it, is not clear to the present compiler from the sources which have been consulted. As an aside, the Chronicles do, in fact, begin with the birth of Christ, but entries from the first five centuries are few and far between, and the information provided by them is understandably very sketchy.

1072 William of Poitiers begins his *Gesta Willielmi ducis Normannorum et regis Anglorium* – the title of which should need no translation! – a book on the life of William the Conqueror.

1073 During this period the Abbot of Tavistock is required to provide and equip 15 knights for the service of the king. A rough idea of the wealth of the abbey can be estimated by comparing this requirement with the wealthy sees of Canterbury and Winchester, whose bishops each have to send 60 knights during any national call to arms.

1074 King William raises an army to fight in Flanders. Perhaps many of the newly-appointed lords of Dartmoor manors, and their followers, sail with him.

1075 After another year of more bloodshed, in-fighting and treachery in Britain, which seems to have continued almost unabated throughout the century, the A-S Chronicles of this year end with a short poetic refrain – "Some were blinded/Some outlawed from the land/And some brought to shame/Thus were traitors to the King/Put down".

1076 The king appoints a commission to investigate the activities of county sheriffs, amongst them some of the leading barons of the time, ordering them to reinstate stolen lands and properties to their rightful owners.

1077 The first 'Great Fire' occurs, 589 years before *the* Great Fire – " ... also ... this year the town of London burnt down one night..." (A-S Chronicles).

1078 "This year was the dry summer...the wildfire came and burnt down many towns" (A-S Chronicles).

1079 The New Forest is decreed a Royal Hunting Ground. Probably the earliest reference to a Royal Forest, it thus forms an important landmark in the history of the enclosure of tracts of land as royal demesne, particularly with respect to the harsh Forest Laws which were imposed at the time.

1080 Bishop Osborne builds a rural palace at Chudleigh.

1081 At about this time the building of three great cathedrals is in progress – Ely, Rochester and York Minster.

1082 Geoffrey becomes Abbot of Tavistock.

1083 A group of monks are murdered in Glastonbury Abbey; it appears that the abbot himself, Thurstan, was the instigator of the assault. ◆ The Inquisito Geldi records the collections of gelds, or land taxes, in the five western counties of England.

1084 This year does not exist in English history! At least, that is what must be supposed, for the Anglo-Saxon Chronicles contain no entries for 1084.

1085 King William orders a full survey of the shires of England. The details are recorded in the Domesday Book which is completed the following year.

1086 From Domesday, the entire population of Devon is estimated at being just 17,434.

1087 A great famine sweeps across the entire country – King William is himself a victim, and dies in Normandy – which prompts one to wonder how accurate a reflection of the situation the Domesday Survey might have remained only a year after it was produced.

1088 Judhel of Totnes, a trusted follower of William I, is accused of treason by William Rufus, banished from the country and his lands sequestrated. Part of his extensive holdings on Dartmoor, the manor of Peter Tavy, is incorporated into the barony of Hurdwick.

1089 Tremors from a small earthquake are felt on Dartmoor and in other parts of Devon.

1090 The A-S Chronicles contain notes of illegal taxes being imposed by the feudal barons, and "many other misfortunes" which the people suffered at the hands of the nobility.

1091 King Malcolm III of Scotland invades England.

1092 The great age of early Norman cathedral-building continues, with the start of those at Lincoln and Chester, and also the founding of an abbey at Tewkesbury.

1093 This year marks the tricentenary of the earliest documented Viking raid on these shores, the sacking of Lindisfarne Church in AD 793.

1094 In about this year (the exact date is uncertain) Richard de Redvers marries Adeliz, daughter of William Peverel of Nottingham – is this the origin of the Peverel element seen in a number of Devon placenames?

1095 The first crusade begins.

1096 William Rufus grants the manor of Walsinton to the abbey of Tavistock. ◆ Josceline de Courtenay, grandfather of the Reginald de Courtenay who came to England in 1152, fights in the crusade to the Holy Land. It was Josceline's father, Athon, who fortified the town of Courtenay in France and gave its name to the family.

1097 Hugh de Flavigny visits London and, although impressed by its physical extent and large population, finds only one thing of particular note to remark upon, commenting on the large numbers of savage dogs prowling the streets around St Paul's graveyard at night, terrorising travellers and passers-by!

1098 King William II is absent from England all year.

1099 Bishop Odo orders the making of the Bayeaux Tapestry. ◆ The 200th anniversary of the death of Alfred the Great.

The Twelfth Century

1100 The hated king, William Rufus, is killed whilst hunting in the New Forest; the real truth about the incident which led to his death has never been discovered.

1101 Richard de Redvers is awarded the baronies of Plympton, Carisbrooke (I.O.W.) and Christchurch (Dorset), plus no less than 180 manors in Devon, and lands elsewhere in the southern counties, thus elevating the family from minor barons and knights to the status of one of the country's leading families almost overnight. (There were, in fact, a number of grants and awards made to de Redvers between 1101 and 1106, so all of the lands were not given with just one stroke of the pen in a single deed.)

1102 Edward the Confessor's tomb is reopened, and the rumour that the body had not decayed found to be true.

1103 Anselm, Archbishop of Canterbury, embarks on a journey to Rome, expected to take around three months to complete.

1104 The 150th anniversary of the formal unification of England after Eric Bloodaxe was killed by King Edred in 954 at Stainmore Pass in the Pennines.

1105 King Henry invades Caen and Bayeux.

1106 The A-S Chronicles record the presence of "an unusual star...in the southwest...little and dark, but the light which stood out from it was bright...", and also state that two moons are seen in the sky before Easter – observations which suggest that strong alcohol was not unknown to the 12th century chroniclers!!

1107 The tower of Winchester Cathedral collapses, damaging William II's tomb.

1108 The 970th anniversary of the death, in AD 138, of Emperor Hadrian.

1109 "This year there was much thunder, very awesome" (A-S Chronicles).

1110 Pipe rolls, records of the sheriffs' accounts etc from each county, from which snippets of Dartmoor's early history can be learnt, are first introduced. Remaining in force until 1834, they are the longest series of English public records.

1111 The (re)building of Exeter Cathedral commences, replacing the poorly constructed edifice which was erected after the original one was destroyed in 1003 (this original building dated to 932).

1112 The 480th anniversary of the death, in AD 632, of Edwin, overlord of South Britain, killed in the Battle of Hatfield.

1113 A group of French monks from Laon, en route from Exeter to Bodmin, are escorted across Dartmoor. Their guide shows them what he calls King Arthur's Chair and Oven, which is perhaps the cairn atop Water Hill – which was to be named as the King's Oven in 1240.

The cairn on Water Hill – 'King Arthur's Chair'? (q.v. 1113).

1114 The 500th anniversay of the Battle of Bampton, Devonians vs Saxons, at which the former lost 2,046 men.

1115 Every year we are nowadays reliably informed by newscasters and reporters etc that the year has seen the worst rainfall, coldest nights, most severe storms, heaviest snowfalls, highest winds, and so on, since records began, and this strangely English preoccupation, with every natural phenomenon being far worse than the one which preceded it, has, it seems, a long history! The A-S Chronicles record that the winter of 1115 was, yet again, so harsh "that no man then living ever remembered one more severe". With all these "more severe" winters piling up one after the other, with amazing regularity, it is a wonder that the country managed to survive into the 12th century, let alone the 21st!

1116 Complaints about taxation are also not a modern phenomenon, as the A-S Chronicles testify, again recording that "this land and the people were this year very often sorely oppressed by the taxes". Nothing has changed – over eight and a half centuries later the people are still being "sorely oppressed" by them!

1117 This year marks the 750th anniversary of the great 'Barbarian Invasion', when, in AD 367, the Roman occupiers were attacked by the Picts, Scots and Saxons.

1118 King Henry I spends the year fighting in Normandy against the forces of the French king and the counts of Anjou and Flanders.

1119 The Order of the Knights Templars is founded.

1120 At about this time (the exact year unknown) tithes on the fisheries of the manor of Buckland Monachorum are granted to Tavistock Abbey.

1121 Sometime in c1667 a lawyer wrote that he had, "after diligent search", found a bundle of ancient deeds, "comencing ano 1121", relating to the manor of Shaugh Prior when it was held by Plympton Priory – where are these deeds now? ◆ One, at least, survives – or a copy of it – naming Brixstanestune (Brixton) in Shaugh Prior and other undefined lands on this side of the River Plym – "que sitra aquam Plime sunt".

1122 Meavy Church is consecrated and dedicated to St Peter.

1123 Guy de Nonant holds the Honour of Totnes, and may well own other ex-Judhel manors in Devon, including some of his Dartmoor properties.

1124 Under the command of King Henry I, English knights, doubtless numbering some of the Devonian barons amongst them, crush an uprising of Norman insurgents at Bourghthéroulde.

1125 Johel de Pomeroy grants the manor of Canonteign to St Mary du Val.

1126 The dawn of a new era in England, perhaps, as one of the last surviving links with the past is severed – the last of the great Saxon overlords is dead. Edgar Atheling, grandson of the Saxon king, Edmund Ironside, had been one of the Saxon lords who offered William of Normandy the crown of England in 1066 after their armies had been defeated in the Battle of Hastings.

1127 To paraphrase a famous remark, "reports of my death have been greatly exagerrated" – Leland records that William Warelwast, Bishop of Exeter and Canon of Plympton Priory, died in this year, thereby 'killing off' the good bishop ten years too early! In his capacity as canon, he is the ultimate owner – or, more correctly, the trustee – of the Dartmoor manors and other lands owned by the priory. His family's coat of arms are to be seen in the church of Plympton St Mary.

1128 As one of the last links with the past is broken (q.v. 1126), the future is being forged. Matilda, daughter of Henry I, marries Geoffrey Plantagenet, Count of Anjou. Through this marriage the Norman kings of England become related to all of the royal blood lines of Europe, including the dukes of Saxony, Burgundy and

Flanders, the counts of Dreux, Castille, Navarre and Toulouse, and the kings of Denmark, France and Prussia. Their son was to become Henry II, King of England, Count of Anjou and Torraine, Duke of Normandy and Acquitaine, and ruler of an Angevin Empire which stretched from the Cheviot Hills to the Pyrenees; head of the most powerful dynasty in Europe and one which was to rule England for 331 years.

(Some of the ancient families of Devon are also related to the early lineage of the counts of Anjou, including those of de Bohun, Bourchier, de Bryonis, Chichester, Courtenay, Ferrers, Prouz, de Redvers and Wrey, amongst a host of others, a list which reads like a 'Who's Who' of some of the most powerful feudal barons of their era...)

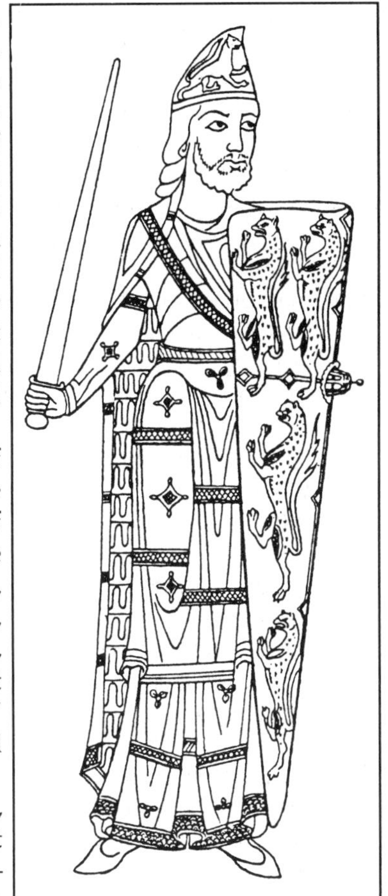

Geoffrey Plantagenet, Count of Anjou (q.v. 1128).
© J. Foster, 1901

1129 ... but, despite their power, prestige and wealth, they did not always get their own way! – Baldwin de Redvers, later to become the Earl of Devon, is fined 500 marks for offences committed within the Royal Forest.

1130 The first church is built atop the 'Rock of Brentor' by Robert Giffard, a lineal descendant of one of the early 11th century dukes of Normandy (q.v. 1006).

1131 King Henry I tries to force his barons to recognise Matilda as his successor.

1132 The building of Fountains and Rievaulx abbeys begins.

1133 Robert le Daneis, lord of Houndtor Manor, Manaton, is one of the signatories to a charter connected with Plympton Priory.

1134 William Creubere is recorded as the owner of Creabere Farm in Tavistock – the earliest documented reference to the Creber family surname.

St Michael of the Rock, the church founded by Robert Giffard (q.v. 1130).

1135 Stephen seizes the English crown, and the Norman-Plantagenet line of English kings is momentarily interrupted. Inter-family rivalry between the counts of Anjou and the Blois line sparks off a bitter war of succession on both sides of the English Channel, which will continue, on and off, for 19 years.

1136 Exeter, held by Baldwin de Redvers of Okehampton, is attacked by King Stephen; the city falls after a three-month siege. ◆ Buckfast Abbey is granted to the Abbot of Sabiny in Normandy.

1137 Ethelward de Pomeroy founds a church in Ashburton.

1138 Robert Chichester becomes Bishop of Exeter.

1139 The civil war continues to rage across England.

1140 Baldwin de Redvers is created Earl of Devon as a reward for his support of Empress Matilda in the war against King Stephen.

1141 Matilda, daughter of King Henry I, briefly reigns as uncrowned monarch until being ousted by Stephen in the following year.

1142 The Plantagenet dynasty, led by Geoffrey Plantagenet (in Normandy) and his wife Matilda (in England), control most of Normandy and the whole of western England. King Stephen, of the Blois line, controls the rest of the country. Many Anglo-Norman Westcountry barons play major roles in helping to secure the Plantagenet stranglehold on Devon, but exact dates and places, to which firm personal names can be assigned, appear to be wanting.

1143 Eustace becomes Abbot of Buckfast.

1144 The civil war continues to rage across England, and a contemporary writer says, of western England, "you could see villages with famous names standing solitary and almost empty". Unfortunately, as is so often the case with these early narratives, none of the "famous names" are actually named!

1145 After this year no Westcountry baron holding extensive lands defects to King Stephen's side. The stalemate, interrupted by occasional battles and sieges, continues for another ten years.

1146 At about this time a Geoffrey de Spineto, probably of the Sampford Spiney family (q.v. 1153), is witness, along with other prominent Devonians, to various grants of lands etc to found Christchurch Priory and Quarr Abbey.

1147 The second crusade begins. ◆ The Savignac Monks of Buckfast Abbey (q.v. 1136) are absorbed into the Cistercian Order.

1148 Empress Matilda leaves England for the final time.

1149 Knights of Devon, and elsewhere, return wearied from the second crusade.

1150 A small chapel is erected on the site of the present church at Shaugh Prior.

1151 Count Geoffrey of Anjou dies.

1152 Reginald de Courtenay arrives in England with Queen Eleanor and later (the exact year is uncertain) marries Hawise, daughter of Robert d'Abrinces, a descendant of the de Bryonis' of the barony of Okehampton. Courtenay thus becomes Baron of Okehampton and hereditary Sheriff of Devon in the right of his wife. The family is destined to become the earls of Devon.

1153 The manor of Sampford is held by Robert de Spinet.

1154 King Stephen dies and the Plantagenets once again regain total control of England and Normandy with the accession of King Henry II, son of Geoffrey and Matilda, who had been waging the war against King Stephen and his followers for 19 long years.

1155 A clerk called Hamelin is referred to in a letter written by Walter Giffard, the earliest reference to the surname – more familiarly spelt Hamlyn – which the compiler of these entries has come across, and a family which was in later centuries to play such an important role in the history of Widecombe and of Buckfastleigh.

1156 The pipe rolls record the earliest reference to tin in Devon.

1157 Richard, later to become King Richard I, Duke of Acquitaine, is born at Oxford. ◆ Richard de Bellomonte succeeds to the manor of Alrichescot (Addiscott) in South Tawton.

1158 £16 13s 4d is paid to the king by the sheriff of North Tawton for "de minaria stagni" – the mining of tin. The rate is the same annually for the following few years, and presumably represents a fixed rent, or rate, paid on the tin extracted from a number of tinworks on north Dartmoor. The sum increases to £20 in 1162 and then to £23 6s 8d (116 marks) in 1164.

1159 A new system of taxation replaces the Danegeld.

1160 Goisten Bastard is the holder of nine manors belonging to the Honour of Plympton.

1161 Hugh de Raleigh is appointed Sheriff of Devon, in which capacity he will serve until 1166.

1162 A deed refers to Hikelake (Hecklake, Whitchurch) as being part of the lands included in the 1130 foundation grant for the building of Brentor Church.

1163 Richard de Redvers, Earl of Devon, dies and is buried at Christchurch, Dorset.

1164 William Fitzralph founds an almshouse for the poor in Exeter.

1165 Westminster Abbey is two centuries old.

1166 A moiety (half) of the Honour of Barnstaple is held by William de Braose. He is the grandson of one of the daughters of Judhel of Totnes, who held extensive lands on Dartmoor (and throughout Devon) after the Conquest.

1167 Roger Abbe pays 10 marks to the king for his right to lands in Peter Tavy and South Milton.

1168 The earliest documented reference to tinworking in the Mewy Valley.

The ruins of the Black Tor blowing house, a post-medieval tin mill built on the site of earlier streamworks in the Mewy Valley (q.v. 1168).

1169 The Anglo-Norman rule of Ireland begins. Many knights with Devonian connections would be Protectors of this part of the realm in the succeeding centuries, including, amongst them, members of the Bourchier and Chichester families.

1170 Thomas à Becket is murdered in Canterbury Cathedral. One of the murderers is William de Tracey, who is later forced to give up the manor of Doccombe, part of his Moretonhampstead estate, to the Dean & Chapter of Canterbury as part of his punishment for his role in the crime.

1171 The 300th anniversary of the Battle of Ashdown, where King Ethelred and his brother, Alfred, defeated the Danes. Ethelred was killed in the battle and was succeeded by Alfred.

1172 Remarkable though it might seem, the basic laws governing the running of the established Church in England are already 500 years old this year, having been formulated at a Great Synod held at Hertford in AD 672.

1173 The 500th anniversary of the birth of the Venerable Bede, whose work on *The Ecclesiastical History of the English Nation* provides such a valuable record of the history of England during the first five centuries after the birth of Christ.

1174 The earliest reference to bull-baiting, which still took place in villages such as Sheepstor and Ashburton as late as the 1830s: it was outlawed in 1835.

1175 At the assize of Northampton, England is divided into six judicial districts, each with its own judges.

1176 Eustachious Fitzstephen is Sheriff of Devon.

1177 A monk steals the bones of St Petroc from Bodmin Priory and takes them to Brittany. Many Westcountry churches are named after the saint, including those at Lydford and South Brent.

1178 Oliver de Tracey inherits the barony of Barnstaple from his father of the same name. Holne Manor and Holne Chase belong to the barony at this time.

1179 The 200th anniversary of the murder of King Edward the Martyr at Corfe Castle.

1180 The last year in which the barons of Devon (and everywhere in England) wielded almost unlimited power through military force as the Assize of Arms of 1181 decrees that all free men should provide themselves with arms commensurate to their status and wealth, the first step which ultimately led to the collapse of the purely feudal system. (Up until 1181 arms were provided by the lords of the manors, the men who thus, by inference, were under the control of the barons.) At the same time, the scutage paid in lieu of knight's service finances a professional standing army for the first time.

1181 The earliest recorded documentary reference to Dartmoor – named as Dertemora – as a distinct region of Devon.

1182 A document of this date is worth mentioning, which, it is understood, is the earliest Final Concord known to exist. It is of related interest to the contents of this book, for it names Ranulf de Glanville, an ancestor of the Tavistock family of that name, as one of the justices of the King's Bench. The fine itself does not relate to Devon, but names properties in St Ivo and Ramsey.

1183 Prince Henry, the young king, dies of a fever.

1184 Glastonbury Abbey is virtually destroyed by fire. Rebuilding begins immediately. ◆ The earliest reference to the Church of St Eustachius, Tavistock, in which year it is granted to the Abbot of Tavistock by John the Chantor, the newly-instituted Bishop of Exeter.

1185 A less common spelling variant of Ashburton is seen for the first time, in a deed which names the place as "Eispreton" – the first element of which is still presumably pronounced as it is in the more familiar variants such as Ayssheberton, Aishpreton etc.

1186 The Bishop of Exeter issues a confirmation of the possessions of

Plympton Priory, amongst which are the manors of Shaugh Prior and Dean Prior.

1187 The Devon barons gather their retainers together and prepare for yet another war against the 'old enemy' on the opposite side of the Channel.

1188 King Henry II leaves these shores for the final time.

1189 Upon becoming king, Richard the Lionheart pays a brief visit to England. Brief visit? – Yes, despite reigning for ten years, Richard spent only seven months in England (he was to pay another short visit in 1194, before leaving again to fight in France). ◆ The third crusade begins.

1190 Ralph de Albini, great x9 grandson of Richard Glunold (q.v. 1029), and father of the first member of the Devon family to take the name Daubeney (q.v. 1045), is killed whilst on crusade at the Siege of Acre. ◆ The 500th anniversary of Boniface's entry into a monastery at Exeter. He was martyred in 754.

1191 Richard Reinell is appointed governor of Exeter Castle and Sheriff of Devon.

1192 Abbotsham Church is appropriated to the abbey of Tavistock.

1193 A charter records that by this year the original holdings of Plympton Priory had been extended by the following lands in and around Dartmoor (as well as many properties and lands elsewhere in Devon) – land in Sampford Spiney, given by Asceline; the churches of Ugborough and Ilsington; lands in Tamerton, given by Alured; Brixton Barton in Shaugh Prior; Watervale, Rowden, Woodmanswell and Langstone, all in Brentor; half the tithe on the fisheries at Bickleigh; and unnamed lands given by Matilda Peverel in exchange for lands in Kilbury in Buckfastleigh (later called the manor of Kilburland).

1194 Roger Foliot bequeaths the tithes of his rents on properties in Throwleigh to Christchurch Priory (Dorset). The reason for the out-of-county bequest is not quite clear, but it points to some relationship between Foliot and the de Redvers family, founders of the priory.

1195 Lydford Castle keep is built at a cost of £32.

1196 An outline pedigree compiled in 1393 traces the ancestry of Prouz of Gidleigh to a Walter Prouz who married a daughter of the Wibbery family in 1196.

1197 William de Wrotham is appointed First Lord Warden of the Stannaries.

1198 Jordan de Lancellis gives Henry de Pomeroy a warhorse in exchange for lands at Cheriton.

1199 John, Earl of Mortaigne (the future king), issues a charter defining

The ruined keep of Lydford Castle (q.v. 1195).

the rights and liberties of the Forest to which the earls, barons, knights, free tenants, clergy and laity in Devon are entitled (this, in fact, merely reconfirmed rights which they already held, and did little to resolve the issues of the day, which eventually resulted in the disafforestation of Devon five years later).

*****

The Thirteenth Century

1200 Osbert Fitzwilliam becomes Sheriff of Devon.

1201 The charter of King John grants free status to the tinners of Devon and Cornwall, making them subject only to the jurisdiction of the Lord Warden of the Stannaries and their courts. Trying to define these rights in precise terms, and identifying who was and who was not entitled to them, would line the pockets of lawyers for the next seven centuries!

1202 Robert de Ilsington becomes Prior of Plympton.

1203 The king grants the city of Exeter to Queen Isabella for life.

1204 The charter disafforesting the county of Devon, except the Forests of "Dertemore" and "Exemore", is signed at Winchester. The 'fine' imposed on the men of Devon for their release from the Forest Laws is 5,000 marks. The bounds of the Forest of Dartmoor are stated to be "as they were in the time of King Henry I", a reference to a deed or charter (or some other record) of the extent of the Forest which has not survived.

1205 Robert de Courtenay pays £500 for the livery of the barony of Okehampton, plus 92 and one-third knight's fees.

1206 Henry Marshall is fined 500 marks for hunting within the Forest, a fine imposed not for the offence of hunting per se, but because he was not one of the Devon knights and other gentry who had, in 1204, paid for the liberty.

1207 Moretonhampstead is granted the right to hold a weekly market. The right was later reconfirmed in a grant issued to Hugh de Courtenay in 1335.

1208 In the Court of Common Pleas at Westminster a Raunulph de Albarmarle claims 40s worth of land in Dene (Dean Prior) and Taui (Mary Tavy), and the moiety of a mill at Taui, in what is perhaps the earliest documented reference to a grist, or corn, mill anywhere on Dartmoor (pre-dating the earliest known references to the mills at Babeny and Buckland-in-the-Moor by nearly a century). Moreover, de Albarmarle produces a deed in support of his claim, confirming a grant of the mill and lands which had been issued to his father, which possibly takes the date of the building back as early as the mid-12th century, sometime c1150.

1209 Reports of the death, in a Ford Abbey Cartulary, of Hawise de Courtenay in this year are greatly exaggerated! In fact, the pipe rolls prove that she was alive in 1211, and even as late as 1214, in which year she paid $7^1/_2$ marks for the Honour of Okehampton. ◆ Reports of the deaths of some others are not exagerrated – 112 pirates are beheaded in a single day on the Island of Tresco! But they do cause some consternation, for the person ultimately responsible for the deaths, as protector of the coastline in his capacity as owner of the Scilly Isles, is the Abbot of Tavistock! A petition to the king to relieve the abbot of this burden, originally granted to Tavistock Abbey in 1114, is refused.

1210 The 500th anniversary of the Battle of Irie, at which Nunna of Sussex fought against Geraint, King of Dumnonia.

1211 Excavations carried out at Dinna Clerks in the 1970s demonstrate that the longhouse was probably built sometime around this year, and abandoned less than a century later when a fire engulfed the building (q.v. 1271).

1212 The overlord of Curnwod and Ludeton (Cornwood and Lutton) is the Earl of Mortain.

1213 Pope Innocent III authorises King Philip of France to invade England to depose King John, but John bows to pressure and the interdict is lifted (imposed in 1208 because of King John's refusal to recognise the papal appointment of Stephen Langton as Archbishop of Canterbury).

1214 The output of tin from Devon and Cornwall reaches a peak at 133,000 cwt, a figure which would not be exceeded for another four centuries. ◆ King John grants the manor of Blackaton to William Pipard, after William de la Forbe had been dispossessed of it.

1215 The Magna Carta is sealed. In connection with Dartmoor history it has particular relevance in one important respect, in that it limited the king's powers to tax the feudal barons (plus, of course, its other clauses affected Dartmoor just as much as they did the rest of the nation).

1216 King John grants Lydford to William Briewere.

1217 A 'Charter Forestae' decrees that three Courts of Swainmote are to be held annually in each Royal Forest. None are known to survive from Dartmoor (the records of later manor courts held at Lydford are not quite the same for, in strict legal conformity, Dartmoor had, by then, become a chase).

1218 William Briewere grants a right to the men of Lady Isabella, the second wife of King John, to dig and carry away peat from Dartmoor for use in her own tin mine, the location of which is not recited in the covenant.

1219 The Sheriff of Devon is commanded to elect "two worthy and discreet knights of the neighbourhood of Dartmoor" to be verderers for the king for the Forest of Dartmoor. ◆ Sheepstor is not the 'tor of sheep', as might be supposed, the modern name being a corrupted form. In this year it is named in a deed as "Shitelestor".

The bold outline of Sheeps Tor dominates the view from the flank of Eylesburrow (q.v. 1219).

1220 Lucy de Alneto conveys her half of the manor of Kideleg (Gidleigh) to William Prouz and Alice de Kideleg.

1221 Waleran Teutonicus becomes Lord Warden of the Stannaries.

1222 King Henry III directs the bailiffs of the manor of Lydford to allow tinners to take fuel (peat) from the moor.

1223 A Martin de Pateshill, or Pateshull, is named as one of the jurors at the Court of Common Pleas at Westminster. The Battishills, or Battishulls, were to become a prominent family in the area around South Tawton, Throwleigh, Gidleigh etc, and perhaps Martin de Pateshill was one of their ancestors.

1224 A perambulation of Dartmoor might have taken place in this year, under the terms of a statute issued for perambulating the Forests of England. ◆ Roger de Tony is permitted to hold pasturing rights on Dartmoor pertaining to his manor of Sutton.

1225 Thomas de Cirencester is ordered to inquire into the value of corn on the manors of Backleg (Bickleigh), Boclond (Buckland Monachorum) and Walthamton (Walkhampton).

1226 A badly mutilated effigy on a tomb inside the church at Atherington, marking the final resting place of Sir William Champerknowne, Knight, is said to date to about this year. The Dartmoor link is but a tenuous one – a later member of the family owned the Maristow Estate in the immediate post-dissolution era, before it was bought by the Slannings of Ley.

1227 The king issues a writ obliging Roger de Tony to permit the market to be held at Lydford "which used to be anciently held there".

1228 John de la Hele is recorded as owner of the Hele Farms in Cornwood.

1229 An Alice de Kideleg and William le Pruz are named in a quitclaim of a moiety of the manor of Kideleg. Suggested by a previous author to be a reference to Little Cadleigh, this, in fact, refers to Gidleigh (q.v. 1220).

1230 Thomas de Cirencester becomes Sheriff of Devon.

1231 Death of the Queen of Navarre, Richard the Lionheart's widow.

1232 Incredible though it might seem to present-day researchers, many of whom are perfectly content to confine their study of original documents to the post-medieval era, the surviving manuscript of the Bede's *Ecclesiastical History of the English Nation* is, by now, already five centuries old!

1233 Barons keen to rid the king of Poitevin influences meet at Oxford.

1234 Richard de Langeford becomes Lord Warden of the Stannaries.

1235 The hundred rolls record that Nicholas de Moelys is Sheriff of Devon. ◆ The Bishop of Exeter is amongst those chosen to escort Isabella, the king's sister, to France for her marriage to Emperor Frederick II.

1236 Robert de Courtenay holds the Honour of Okehampton in 92½ knight's fees (185 marks).

1237 The king grants the tithe of herbage in the Forest to St Petroc's Church, Lydford.

1238 Henry III grants the Forest of Dartmoor to his brother Richard, Earl of Poitou and Cornwall.

1239 Richard pays rent of £10 for his rights in the Forest.

1240 The Perambulation of Dartmoor. Writing almost seven centuries later, William Crossing gives a superb account of the proceedings in his *Echoes of an Ancient Forest,* transporting his readers back in time and conducting them on the perambulation in the company of the twelve knights and the throng of followers, including, amongst them, some of the local peasants and worthies who gathered to take part in this unique event in the annals of Dartmoor's long history.

1241 A map of England in Matthew Paris' *Chronica Majora,* published by the St Alban's Abbey chronicler in about this year, places Devonia north of Dorset and Sumset. ◆ The manor of Throwleigh is held by Fulk de Ferrers.

1242 Hugh Peverel becomes lord of the manor of Stowford. He was to

The Longstone on Shovel Down, one of the ancient bondmarks of the Forest of Dartmoor (q.v. 1240).

die 20 years later, whereupon the manor passed to his son, James.

1243 Michael de Spickewyck is one of the commissioners of the Haytor hundred.

1244 John Fitz Richard holds Blakedune (Blackaton, Widecombe) for ½ knight's fee. ◆ The Abbot of Buffestre (Buckfast) grants William de Sancto Stephano common of pasture and turbary on all the lands in the manor of La Dene (Dean Prior).

1245 Richard de Teynton is granted some land at Forsham, an outlier of the manor of Drewsteignton, for which he must pay Hugh de Dimestorie a pair of white gloves annually at Easter.

1246 Queen Isabella, King John's widow, dies.

1247 Richard, Earl of Cornwall, holds Exeter Castle by this year (seized by the king from Robert de Courtenay in 1232).

1248 Nicholas de Wiltes is instituted rector of Throwleigh.

1249 Hole in Chagford is owned by John de la Hulle.

1250 Hugh de Courtenay, son of John, Baron of Okehampton, is born. His main 'claim to fame' would come in 1288 when, after quarrelling with the monks at Ford Abbey, he raided their cattle and drove them onto Dartmoor.

1251 The original twelve-arched bridge at Exeter is built by Walter Gervis. It was destroyed in a violent flood in 1449.

1252 The passion for hunting in the Royal Forests is carried to extremes in the mid-13th century – in this year Richard of Cornwall kills 32 bucks in just nine days' hunting at Rockingham. Doubtless the Forest of Dartmoor sees many a chase during this period.

1253 Adam Wymer becomes Lord Warden of the Stannaries.

1254 Walter de Chaumberleng assigns a tenement and ½ a ploughland in Belestan (Belstone) and the demesnes, homages, services of free men, villainages, wards, reliefs, escheats, meadows, pastures, woods, waters, mills and appurtenances to Robert de Bello Campo.

1255 Ralph de Baucombe becomes the tenant of the rector of Plympton at a property in Ugborough – presumably the origin of the name Bowcombe, latterly a farm in that parish. The following year another part of the same tenement is granted to another Baucombe as a gift, in return for which the grantee gives "one sore sparrowhawk".

1256 Richard de Spekecote holds ¼ part of the manor of Bellestan (Belstone).

1257 Bishop Bronescombe, upon becoming Bishop of Exeter, holds an inquisition at Buckfast Abbey. The leading men of Devon who, after the death of his predecessor, Bishop Brondy, had forged letters conferring his lands and property etc upon themselves and others, confess and are absolved.

1258 Elias de Hertforde is rector at Walkhampton, the earliest known reference to a church (or chapel?) there.

1259 Bishop Bronescombe again visits Buckfast Abbey.

1260 Bishop Bronescombe grants a dispensation to the inhabitants of the ancient tenements of Babeny and Pizwell allowing them to use Widecombe Church instead of having to make the long trek across Dartmoor to their own parish church at Lydford.

Pizwell, one of the oldest of the ancient tenements of the Forest (q.v. 1260).

1261 Bishop Bronescombe dedicates two churches on Dartmoor, that at Lydford, recently rebuilt, to St Petroc, and Chagford to St Michael.

1262 Ralph de Oddiscumb becomes Lord Warden of the Stannaries.

1263 King Henry III grants all the gold, silver, copper, lead and other metaliferous mines in Devon to Adam de Greynvill and John Silvester.

1264 Hugh Peverel becomes Lord Warden of the Stannaries.

1265 The earliest known reference to the unusually-named St Eustachius in Tavistock, a dedication it shares with only two other English churches.

1266 Even more unusual is that of Chittlehampton Church (where Robert de Stanweye is the rector), whose dedication is unique – to St Hieritha. She also appears on the screen at Hennock Church, on the eastern edge of Dartmoor.

1267 Peter de Plymstoke is instituted vicar of Dean Prior.

1268 Lydford is granted the right to hold a market on Wednesdays and a three-day fair on the feast of St Petroc.

1269 Robert le Deneys is given a gift of one ploughland and one messuage in Manaton in return for the peppercorn rent of "one clove gillyflower at Easter for all service, custom and exaction", to be paid yearly to Robert Knoel, on whose behalf le Deneys is also to perform suit of service to the manor courts.

1270 William de Fuleford grants 1/4 part of Belstone Manor to Richard Corbyn.

1271 Upon the resignation of Sir William de Sancti Martina (in 1270), Master Henry de Hamptesfort becomes rector of Petrockstowe Church. Patrons of the living are the abbot and convent of Buckfast Abbey. ◆ The head of the household at Dinna Clerks possibly loses a penny in this year. Yes, seriously! – a penny from the reign of King Edward III was found in the ruined longhouse during excavations carried out in the 1970s, along with the charred remnants of a large number of other artefacts hurriedly abandoned when the building was totally destroyed by a fire sometime c1300.

1272 Bishop Bronescombe commits the custody of the church at Lydford to Adam de Bremelle, chaplain.

1273 The Cistercian abbey at Buckland is founded by Amicia, Countess of Devon.

1274 William de Boclond becomes one of the "Twelve Sworn men of the Haytorre Hundred".

1275 Ralph de Cheverston, the bailiff of the Forest of Dartmoor, doubles the agistment fees of the Forest to 1d for an ox and 2d for a horse.

1276 A document of this date, its authenticity perhaps debatable (at least, it is to the present compiler), apparently cites that the Abbot of Bufestre (Buckfast) holds the manor of Sele Monachorum as a gift from King Canute – could this be the key to the suggestion that the abbey was 'founded' by Canute? (q.v. 1030).

1277 William de Albermarle holds the manor of Leweneston by the service of "two arrows and an oat cake when the King should be in Dartmoor".

1278 The 400th anniversary of the Battle of Edington, which took place after the Danes had deceived Alfred into believing that they were to relinquish their hold on Exeter and Wareham.

1279 The Statute of Mortmain stops landowners giving land to the church in order to avoid paying fuedal dues.

1280 A survey of the manor of Gidleigh records that it comprises a capital messuage worth 4s p.a., 60 acres of arable land worth 10s, 30 acres of scrub and pasture worth 3s 4d, "a certain waste" worth 6s 8d, two mills worth 26s 8d, sixty free tenants who pay £4 3s [total] and forty villagers who hold $^1/_2$ ferling of land each and who pay £3 at Michaelmas.

1281 Richard de la Stenylake is involved in an incident in a nearby tinwork in which a tinner is killed (the property referred to is the now abandoned and ruinous farmstead of Stenlake in Walkhampton).

The ruins of Stenlake Farm, at, or near, the site where Richard de la Stenylake lived seven centuries ago (q.v. 1281).

1282 Baldwin Speccot, who had previously taken the surname de Belston after the name of the manor which he held (and still holds), is summoned to prove his rights to hold a view of frankpledge (court leet) at Parkham. He proves his right, which he holds under the baronage of Okehampton.

1283 Bishop Quivil, Bishop of Exeter, visits the manor of Ashburton. ◆ Roger le Rous sells some land in Widecombe to the parish, later to become the glebe land, upon which still stands the glebe house and its associated buildings (opposite the church house in the square).

1284 In connection with a donation to Exeter Cathedral, made by Roger le Rous of Wydecomb, is a reference to a St Leonards Chapel in Spitchwick, the exact location of which is unknown to the present compiler (but possibly at, or near, the site of the present Leusdon Church which is, in fact, situated in Spitchwick Manor, Widecombe).

1285 Letters Patent authorise Serlo de Lanladron to assign Widecombe Church to the Dean & Chapter of Exeter.

1286 William Pipard dies seized of the manors of Blaketon and North

Bovey.

1287 A hundred roll records that at about this time "Margery Pipard had gallows and an assize of bread and beer within the manor of North Bovey and her ancestors had enjoyed these privileges from time immemorial, but no man can tell by what warrant".

1288 Olditch, near South Zeal, is occupied at this time by Geoffrey de la Yolledeche, the 'old ditch' in the personal and property name said to refer to an ancient bank and ditch nearby, marking the border of the Forest; but probably intended to mark the limits of the commons (i.e. the purlieus of the Forest), rather than the Forest of Dartmoor itself.

1289 Stephen de Haccombe owns the manor of Combe Hall in Drewsteignton.

1290 The pipe rolls record the payment of £77 2s 4¼d in dues on 87,785lbs of tin produced in Devon.

1291 Perhaps the earliest documented reference to what was later to become Yelverton, which in this year is just a small farm called Elleford. ◆ Robert Champeaux, Abbot of Tavistock, is one of the founders of Gloucester College, Oxford. From henceforth Tavistock Abbey always maintained a student at the college at its own expense.

1292 The Courtenays inherit the barony of Okehampton following the death of Isabella de Fortibus.

1293 Scorriton is named in a deed of this year as "Scoryaton juxta Bukfast".

1294 Wool merchants and producers in Devon, and throughout the nation, are hit with the 'Maltote', an export tax of 40s per sack imposed upon them.

1295 Sir William Prouz, builder of the fortified manor house at Gidleigh, which was to be later known as Gidleigh Castle, becomes MP for Devon.

1296 Huccaby, named as Woghebye, becomes the third of the ancient tenements to be documented. The original name is thought to mean 'crooked bend', a reference to the wide sweep of the River Dart above the settlement. ◆ There are 5,000 head of cattle, 487 horses and 131 folds of sheep depastured within the bounds of the Forest.

1297 King Edward I visits Buckfast Abbey.

1298 Ashburton is represented in Parliament for the first time.

1299 Thomas de Doune holds two messuages and three ploughlands in "Leye next Spikeswyck" (Leighon near Spitchwick).

*****

The Fourteenth Century

1300 Sir Hugh de Courtenay of Okehampton is one of the English knights who fights in the Battle of Caerlaverock.

1301 This is the century in which are found the earliest references to many of the ancient tenements of the Forest. Babbeneye and Pushylle (Babeny and Pizwell) had been named in 1260, and Woghebye (Huccaby) in 1296, and the next 'oldest' is Walna, referred to by this name in 1301.

1302 The building of Babeny corn mill probably commences in this year, for a document of 1303 records it as having been "newly built".

1303 The earliest surviving coinage roll for Devon, listing tin assayed at the three original stannary towns, records that $17\frac{1}{2}$ tons of tin are coined at Chagford; Ricardus de Middleworthi pays 6s $10\frac{1}{4}$d on his tin coined at Ashburton.

1304 John Pipard holds the manor of North Bovey for $\frac{1}{2}$ knight's fee.

1305 The rectory of Walkhampton is appropriated to Buckland Abbey. ◆ Earliest known reference to the ancient tenement of Donebrugge (Dunnabridge).

1306 Because the old vicarage at Sowton is too far from Churchtown (Buckland Monachorum village), a new one is ordered to be built at Lowercombe.

1307 The ancient tenement of Sherberton gets its earliest mention in this year, as too does that of Bremst (Brimpts).

1308 Henry Cole is Portreeve of Okehampton.

1309 Bishop Stapledon obtains a charter from the king for a Saturday fair at Ashburton, and an annual fair on St Laurence's Day, August 11th.

1310 Sticklepath Bridge is repaired at a cost of 13s 10d.

1311 Henry de Lacey grants the manor of Holne, "except 3,000 acres of wood and the advowson of the church", to William Martyn. ◆ The Abbot of Buckland is given a plot of land on the north side of Walkhampton Church upon which to build a tithe barn.

1312 Piers Gaveston, to whom the Forest of Dartmoor had been granted by Edward II, suddenly finds himself out of favour and loses his head over it (!). Thomas L'Ercedekne becomes custodian of the Forest of Dartmoor, and places it under the charge of Thomas de Sherigge.

1313 Henry Bloyou, rector of Cornwood, is charged with entering

William Martyn's warren in Ugborough in pursuit of hares and rabbits, and has his revenues sequestrated to the value of two marks by the bishop's court at Exeter.

1314 A grammar school is founded in Ashburton by Bishop Stapleton.

1315 Symon de Wibbebury gives his manor of Chaggeforde (Chagford), with the "vasto in more de Dertemore", to Oliver de Wybbebury and his wife, Isolda.

Looking across Green Combe to Jursdon Down, part of the "vasto in more de Dertemore" belonging to Chagford Manor (q.v. 1315).

1316 Arable land in William le Prutz's manor of Gyddelegh (Gidleigh) is valued at just 2d (less than 1p) per acre.

1317 Monks establish a fair at Buckland Abbey. ◆ The earliest documentary references to the ancient tenements of Renewych (Runnage) and Hextenesworthy (Hexworthy).

1318 A suit is brought against the Abbot of Buckland for illegally hunting over the Dartmoor lands of Hugh de Audley. In the following year, doubtless as a snipe at the abbot, the rights are granted to the Abbot of Tavistock.

1319 The Church of St Michael of the Rock, Brentor, is rebuilt by Tavistock Abbey as a chapelry and rededicated by Bishop Stapeldon. ◆ The Forest is granted to Hugh de Audley, Earl of Gloucester, who had married Margaret, Gaveston's widow (q.v. 1312). The grant is for the term of the life of the Countess Margaret (who also happens to be the niece of King Edward II), although the actual custodianship of the Forest is placed in the hands of a number of others during this period.

1320 Thomas Newbegyn delivers the 1204 charter of King John to the Bishop of Exeter for him to examine. Rightly believing it to be a most important document, the bishop copies it into his register under the title "Carta de Libertatibus Devonie".

1321 The rectory of Whitchurch is converted to a chapelry. ◆ Simon Belde and Gilbert de la Forde become Lords Warden of the Stannaries.

1322 Humphrey de Bohun is killed in the Battle of Boroughbridge. It was through the marriage of his daughter, Margaret, to Hugh de Courtenay of Okehampton that the latter family inherited the Powderham Estate.

1323 A terrier of Ugborough Church, compiled in 1927, records that the earliest surviving fabric in the aisles of the nave dates from this year (and that in the chancel from 1420, the tower from 1520).

1324 Philip de Valle Torta holds ten messuages, two ploughlands and $^1/_6$ knight's fee in Chadelwode (Chaddlewood, Plympton St Mary).

1325 John de Beaumond grants the manor of Ingsdon (Ilsington) to William Barry.

1326 Stapleton, sometime Bishop of Exeter, is set upon by a mob in London, who drag him from his horse, strip him and execute him on the spot, later parading his head around the streets on a pole.

1327 Richard Caleware is granted the bailiwick of the Forestership of Dartmoor.

1328 Thomas de Shirygg becomes Lord Warden of the Stannaries, but is replaced later the same year by Richard Caleware. ◆ Plympton is added to Ashburton, Chagford and Tavistock as a stannary town. ◆ Sir John L'Ercedekne succeeds the de Boclandes as owner of the manor of Buckland-in-the-Moor. ◆ Robert de Middlecote is arraigned for a murder said to have been committed in the Chapel of la Wallen at Gidleigh.

1329 William de Moelys holds the manors of Lustelegh, Guddeleghe and Throulegh (Lustleigh, Gidleigh and Throwleigh). ◆ The death of Robert de Elleforde, the king's falconer. A member of a Staffordshire family of this name, it is not clear how, or even if, his ancestry ties into that of the Elfords of Peter Tavy, Sheepstor and Cornwood.

1330 William de Montacute becomes Lord Warden of the Stannaries.

1331 An early reference to the personal name Drogo (though as a forename) in Drewsteignton, in a deed which records that Drogo le Ryche – who might, perhaps, have been moderately wealthy! – claims against William de Merton the rights to one messuage, one ferling of land and four acres of meadow situated in Teyngton Dreu.

The ruins of the tiny Chapel of la Wallen, scene of a brutal murder (q.v. 1328).

1332 The first service is held in the la Wallen Chapel in Throwleigh, newly built after the 1328 murder in the chapel of the same name at Gidleigh. ◆ William de Mewy becomes the vicar at Hatherleigh – its church had been granted to Tavistock Abbey in AD 981, and so the abbot appointed all of its vicars until the dissolution.

1333 Robert Bakere is owner of Puttekesham (Higher Pudsham) in Buckland-in-the-Moor. His direct descendant (through marriages in the 17th century – Baker, Chrispin and Ellis lines), one Thomas Ellis, is owner of the same farm in 1807, in which year it finally loses its independent freehold status upon its sale to the manor.

1334 The chapel at Sampford Spiney is handed over to Plympton Priory.

1335 Robert Michel is Portreeve of Ashburton, the earliest known person to have held this office in the borough.

1336 Cornwood Church is enlarged to one with three altars and rededicated to St Michael by Bishop Grandisson. ◆ The Abbot of Buckland and others, in a "riotous assembly", seize the vicarage of Sutton.

St Michael's, Cornwood, dedicated by Bishop Grandisson (q.v. 1336).

1337 The manor of Lydford and the Forest of Dartmoor is granted by Edward III to Edward, the Black Prince, who becomes the first Duke of Cornwall (the Duchy had formerly been an Earldom, q.v. 1238).

1338 Bishop Grandisson annexes the church of Ilsington to the collegiate church of Ottery St Mary, for which Plympton Priory is from henceforth to receive £5 per annum in compensation

(Ilsington had been a possession of Plympton since its foundation charter of 1121).

1339 The earliest documented reference to serge-making at Horrabridge, at what was later to become known as The Factory (today called Sampford House) in the Springfield area of the village.

1340 Richard atte Thyvele is registered as the owner of Thule in Gidleigh.

1341 Robert de Bourchier becomes Chancellor of England. The Bourchier arms, quartered with those of Wrey, Plantagenet and de Bohun, may be seen on a memorial tablet in Holne Church.

The Wrey – Bourchier – Plantagenet – de Bohun quarterings displayed on a memorial tablet in Holne Church (q.v. 1341).

1342 John Daberman is appointed "Constable of the Castle of Lydford and Custos of the Forest of Dartmoor" under the Black Prince.

1343 John Helston is the reeve of Lydford Burough, John Brownyng the reeve of Dartmoor.

1344 William Pipard of Blakedon Pipard (or Blackadon Piper) becomes High Sheriff of Devon. ◆ Meriputt, the ancient tenement, gets its first mention. The nearby tenement of Dury is also named in the deed.

1345 Two generations of Courtenays take part in the Siege of Calais, which lasts from 1345 until 1348 – Sir Hugh, Knight of the Garter, son of Sir Hugh de Courtenay (deceased), Earl of Devon, High Admiral of the West Seas and Baron of Okehampton, and two of his sons: another Hugh, heir to the barony and earldom (he was to be created a knight after the end of the siege), and Sir Philip of Powderham, Lord Lieutenant of Ireland and Steward of Cornwall. The basic Courtenay arms, "Or three torteaux", are borne on three standards, and to distinguish themselves from each other in the heat of battle, the differencing mark of "a label of three charged with as many crescents of the field" is borne by Sir Hugh senior, "a label of five charged with a fleur-de-lys argent" signifies his elder son, Hugh, whilst Sir Philip's followers rally to a banner bearing "a label of five charged with a plate". The coats of arms of many other Devon gentry families are also carried into battle at Calais.

1346 John de Alneto dies seized of the manors of Cornwood, Gidleigh and Throwleigh. ◆ Ralph Daubeney is one of a number of Devon knights to fight at Creçy.

1347 Earliest reference to the ancient tenement of Lakehead. ◆ A roll of the Black Torrington hundred records that two members of the de Belston family, lords of the manor of that name, pay just 6d ($2^1/_2$p) each a year in tax!

1348 Richard de Mewy's and Walter de Mewy's manor of Weldraden (Walreddon) comprises four messuages, two mills, one dovecot, four ploughlands, 30 acres of meadow, 20 acres of woodland and 200 acres of furze and heath. ◆ The Black Death lays waste half of Europe, and Dartmoor does not escape untouched.

1349 The Earl of Warwick grants the advowson and rectory of South Tawton to the College of St George, Windsor, which remains patron of the living to the present day.

1350 Bartholomew de Burghersh becomes Lord Warden of the Stannaries.

1351 Amongst the properties in the Forest which the bailiff records as being unoccupied in this year are Edithull, Walebrook, Brantclive, Algarslake, Black Staith and Blackfursses.

1352 Labourers are no longer free to seek work where they will – the Statute of Labourers Act, which came onto the statute books during the previous year, restricts the movement of peasants from their native manors and keeps wages at their pre-plague rates.

1353 The king grants John de Belston, holder of Belstone in fee of honour from Okehampton, life exemption from "being put on assizes, juries, or recognitions, and from appointment as mayor, sheriff, coroner, or other bailiff".

1354 The Black Prince orders his Foresters to live continually on the moor in calving-time, to protect the "tender calves" from the herdsmen who patrol the wastes looking after the cattle in their care (the calves referred to are deer calves). ◆ Robert de Eleford succeeds John Daberman as constable of Lydford Castle.

1355 Welford (Bellever) gets its first mention as one of the ancient tenements of the Forest.

1356 John Fox is reeve of the manor of Shaugh Prior.

1357 The Black Death having passed, life is now returning to normal on Dartmoor, and empty farms and cottages have already been reoccupied by new tenants. ◆ John de Courtenay pays 2,500 marks for the wardship of the heirs of John de Neville – an astronomical sum for the time (1 mark = 13s 4d = 66p), it is almost impossible to envisage what the present equivalent would be in pure monetary terms.

1358 John Balancer and Walter Goldbeter lease all the gold, silver and copper mines in Devon from the king; the rent is 20 marks for the first year, then a fifth of the profits from ore raised every year thereafter.

1359 Richard Gold pays 2d rent for two acres of land "between Wallbrook bound and Renwyth" (between Wallabrook and Runnage). ◆ The Abbot of Buckland complains to the king that the latter's Foresters invaded the bounds of his manor of Walkhampton to collect estrays.

1360 Richard, sometime Bishop of Armagh, dies in Avignon. It has been suggested, on what evidence or authority the present compiler has been unable to ascertain, that he was born in Widecombe.

1361 Richard of Southeton grants all of his lands in Tavistock to John of Mewy, a possible reference to the present Sowtontown in Peter Tavy parish.

1362 Abraham Eliot pays 6d rent for two acres of land at Dowbridge Ford and a parcel of land at Sherborne (Dunnabridge Ford and Sherberton); John Northway pays 1½d for an acre of land at Laddretorre (Lough Tor).

1363 Because few ordinary people of the country speak or read French (the language of the gentry, and that used in the courts), and cannot understand what is being said for or against them in pleadings (and often do not even know the laws themselves), all pleas in court are from henceforth to be conducted in English. The Act which brings this law onto the statute books is written in French!!

1364 John Russel pays William and Alice Fot ten marks of silver for a messuage and garden in Tavistock. Somewhat lower in the social heirarchy than the later Russells, Earls of Bedford, with which the town was to become closely associated, this John Russel is a humble cook.

1365 John Glanville of Tavistock is amongst the English knights who sail to Spain with Edward, the Black Prince.

1366 Richard Totewill issues a quitclaim to William Dymmock confirming his ownership of five messuages, one dovecot, two carucates of land, 12 acres of meadow, 12 acres of woodland and 14d rent in Harford and Loudebrok (Lud Brook) in Ugborough, and in the neighbouring parishes.

1367 The Black Prince embarks on an expedition to Castille with 3,000 men-at-arms.

1368 Walter Stonhewar occupies two acres of land at Chiteford, for which he pays 3d p.a. to the bailiff of the Forest.

1369 Edward III resumes the title of King of France.

1370 Abbot Stephen applies to the burgesses of Tavistock for alms to repair and maintain "the grete stone bridge adjoining the towne of Tavystoke".

1371 In an unexpected departure from the normal course of events, peace occurs between England and France – this lasts until 1372!

1372 William Ryka (or Ryks) of Ashburton supplies the tin for the founding of the clock bell of Exeter Cathedral, a total of 617 pounds @ 2d per lb (the copper for the bell is supplied by a John Braysier of Dartmouth).

1373 The manor of Canonteign passes from the Pomeroys to the Chudleighs upon the death of the last of the male line, Sir Henry Pomeroy. (His niece, Joan, sole heiress to the estate, had earlier married James Chudleigh.)

1374 The Abbot of Buckfast is granted a licence to perform services in the chapel atop Brent Hill, South Brent. ◆ Sourton Church is re-dedicated to St Thomas à Becket.

1375 John Cary becomes Lord Warden of the Stannaries.

1376 The Black Prince, first Duke of Cornwall, dies. ◆ A suit is brought by parishioners of Sourton, complaining about the lack of services in their church in winter time – "when sudden inundations of the waters frequently happen the aforesaid inhabitants of Sourton cannot go to the Church of Brydestowe without great difficulty and danger to their persons". Seven centuries later little has changed – the area is still frequently visited by "sudden inundations of water"!

1377 The population of Devon, estimated from the poll-tax returns, is 45,635. ◆ Adam Cole of Slade Manor is assigned to protect the Devon coast from French raiders.

1378 In one of the more unusual cases brought before the Lydford courts, John Kedding is charged with bringing a scythe into the Forest to mow meadows earlier in the year than he should, contrary to the Forest customs.

1379 John Semer is bailiff for the Maristow Estate.

1380 Thomas Mewy is lord of the manors of Mewy and de la Knolle (Knowle).

1381 Richard de Abberbury, granted custody of the Forest in 1377, brings a suit claiming a right to the venville rents as well as the agistment fees.

1382 An inquisition held at Lydford sets out the terms and conditions under which the Fines Villarum (venville rents) had been paid "from the time whereof memory is not", in one of the earliest

The farmhouse at Knowle, now a private dwelling, built on the site of the ancient manor house (q.v. 1380).

references to that well-known principle of 'Time Out of Mind', much beloved by manor courts everywhere, and also used to good effect by some of those who were brought before them and charged with various misdemeanours.

1383 Archbishop William Courtenay, en route to Plympton Priory, dines with the rector of Ugborough. Perhaps one of the after-dinner subjects raised is the fact that the rector had earlier in the year been sued by the priory for rent arrears to the tune of 48 marks. The result of the suit, and whether or not the arrears were paid, does not appear to have been recorded.

1384 The earliest documented reference to the now ruined Norsworthy Farm, near Burrator Reservoir, occurs in this year (named as Northisworthy).

1385 Richard Ruyhale becomes Lord Warden of the Stannaries.

1386 Reginald Strepa becomes one of the churchwardens at St Eustachius, Tavistock.

1387 Henry, later to become King Henry V, is born at Monmouth Castle.

1388 John Coppleston becomes Lord Warden of the Stannaries. ◆ An inquisition into pasturing rights on the commons and in the Forest effectively abolishes the system of "Foldage", which had neatly circumvented the ancient Forest Laws forbidding overnight depasturing – and had also helped to line the pockets of the

Foresters for a few years!

1389 Warin Waldegrave becomes Lord Warden of the Stannaries.

1390 Lead from Lydford Church is ordered to be removed for the repair of castles in Cornwall. ◆ John Scudamore, lord of Shittistore (Sheepstor), grants a property or parcel of land in the parish to Richard Middleworry – could this be a reference to Middleworthy Farm? The document is of greater significance as being the earliest reference to the Scudamores being lords of Sheepstor. Before 1390, a Herbert de Cumba is referred to as being the lord of the manor, at a date unknown.

1391 The 400th anniversary of the Battle of Maldon, which is almost where the notes in this book began. For this marked the first Danish victory over the English in nearly a century, and prompted renewed Viking raids on a more regular basis, ultimately leading to the raids of 997 which were noticed in the opening remarks in the first entry in this book.

1392 Chaucer writes his *Canterbury Tales* at about this time.

1393 The final year of Sir Philip Courtenay's term as Lord Lieutenant of Ireland, a post which he had held since 1383.

1394 Chaucer is granted a £20 annual pension by the king.

1395 This year might mark the 400th anniversary of the founding of the first church on the site of Durham Cathedral, for in 995 a group of exiled monks from Lindisfarne arrived in Durham and built "a little church of wands and branches".

1396 Horebrygge, "on the road between Barum and Plymouth", is repaired.

1397 The manors of South Tauton and Sele (South Zeal) are valued at a combined total of £5 2s 9d in rents.

1398 The Duke of Exeter is one of the noblemen appointed to a newly-formed parliamentary committee to examine and answer petitions etc sent to the king.

1399 John de Waterton becomes Lord Warden of the Stannaries. ◆ A very early reference to 'Lydford Law' (of which Browne later wrote) occurs in a poem written by an anonymous author, said to have been penned in this year – "Now be the law of Lydfford. In londe ne in water". ◆ The manor of Dartmoor (q.v. 1404) is granted to Philip de Courtenay.

*****

The Fifteenth Century

1400 Sometime around this year a branch of the Wrey family of North and South Tawton changes its name to Wyke, after North Wyke, the manor house in which they live.

1401 Richard Mewy and his wife, Matilda, obtain permission from the Bishop of Exeter to hold services in a private chapel at Walreddon, Whitchurch.

1402 John Wyke of North Wyke is Sheriff of Devon.

1403 The Abbot of Buckland leases to John Gey "some land by the ways at Roborough and a parcel at Bycombe at Colverparkysande atte Wateryngge near the land of the Prior of Plympton".

1404 What had in recent years come to be styled the "manor of Dartmoor" again reverts to its former, correct, title of the "manor of Lydford" in the manor courts, styled "Curia legalis manerii de Lydford" (Law court of the manor of Lydford).

1405 One of the earliest references to the tenement at Smallacombe in Sheepstor comes in a deed of this year, which records Martha and Joan Vere as the occupiers, holding rights of common over Rydemoredon and Eyllesburgh (Ringmoor Down and Eylesbarrow).

The western flank of Ringmoor Down, over which the occupiers of Smallacombe held their pasturing rights (q.v. 1405).

1406 A shilling (5p) is given by the Bishop of Exeter towards the rebuilding of Buckfast Bridge.

1407 Thomas Seryneyn surrenders his lease of Wytheparke in Shaugh Prior to the Abbot of Buckland.

1408 The Battle of Bramham Moor.

1409 A millennial anniversary falls this year! – a thousand years ago Britons finally broke free from Roman rule...

1410 ...the last of the Romans fled the country a thousand years ago, but some of them considerately buried their gold hordes for later Britons to rediscover!

1411 The abbey church at Tavistock raises an extra 12s (60p) for its funds by selling ten goats from the parish stock.

1412 Parliament orders a reduction in the weight of coins "because of the great scarcity of money at this time within the realm of England".

1413 John Willecotes becomes Lord Warden of the Stannaries. ◆ A violent flood destroys Holne Bridge on the River Dart, the rebuilding of which begins later in the year.

Holne Bridge on the River Dart (q.v. 1413).

1414 William Burleston conveys the manor of Lustleigh to Sir John Wadham, in whose family it will remain until 1609.

1415 Sir John Chichester is one of just a handful of English knights to fight at Agincourt – his 7x great grandaughter would marry William Bastard, lord of the manor of Buckland-in-the-Moor; his direct descendant, Robert Guy Incledon Chichester, killed in

Flanders in 1914 whilst serving with the Scots Greys, is commemorated in Drewsteignton Church.

1416 For his renewed invasion of France the king borrows money from the noblemen of the nation, and others. John Copleston takes £573 6s 8d to London for the king, the sum loaned by the men of Devon, amongst them the abbots of Buckfast and Tavistock.

1417 Many hundreds of mysterious names appear in the Bailiffs' and Foresters' accounts of the Forest. In this year reference is made to a plot of land, just two acres in extent, "between Pollarde's Wall leyn and Bidegrip and Dart".

1418 In his will, Richard Penels, rector of Moreton, leaves 100s (£5) to the poor of the town, so that they might "pray for his soul". One of his descendants would marry into the Strode family of Newnham Park, and the Pennalls coat of arms is seen in a multiple quartered shield on the tomb raised to Sir William Strode, Knight, in the church at Plympton St Mary.

1419 William Bourchier, ancestor of the Bourchier Wreys, lords of the manor of Holne, is the Count of Ewe, in Normandy. Sometime around this period he marries Anna, daughter of Thomas de Woodstock, the son of King Edward III. ◆ Richard Whittington is Lord Mayor of London for the third time.

1420 Bishop Lacy's register contains the earliest reference to a church at Buckland-in-the-Moor.

1421 The Abbot of Buckland lets land in Attebroke (in Shaugh Prior?) to William Gebbe for 65 years at 7s 7d p.a., the latter to perform suit of service to the manor courts at Horrabridge, and also an annual stint repairing the abbot's fisheries and weirs at Bickleigh.

1422 Bishop Lacy grants a new licence to Elizabeth Raleghe for the newly renovated private chapel at Fardel Manor. ◆ John Copleston and Thomas Congreve become Lords Warden of the Stannaries, to be replaced the following year by Lewis Johan. ◆ William Caxton is born.

1423 The death of Richard Whittington. ◆ William Bonvill is Sheriff of Devon.

1424 Richard Shellebere of Little Torre is brought before the Lydford court charged with blocking a highway at Little Torre called the Moor Way, leading to the Forest.

1425 The manor of Lydford and Forest of Dartmoor are leased to Philip Courtenay and Walter Hungerford for seven years at £105 a year, a grant which was later renewed and then extended for life terms (q.v. 1451).

1426 William Bampfield of Poltimore becomes Sheriff of Devon, replacing Thomas Brooke.

1427 William Beaghe remains Abbot of Buckfast amidst mounting discontent and charges of corruption and immorality. He was finally forced to resign in 1432.

1428 The Fulfords take possession of the manor of Belstone. The first of the new lords (or perhaps his son of the same name?), Baldwin Fulleforde, is some years later accused of being a "rebel, attainted of high treason", and is beheaded after the Battle of Hexham.

1429 The Duke of Gloucester's title as Lord Protector of England is abolished.

1430 Yet more mysteries for present generations of researchers to resolve (q.v. 1417) – in this year 2d rent is being paid to the Forest court for a plot of land said to be situated "at Jockett's mear".

1431 William Ayshe is brought before Chagford court for assaulting Simon Carsleghe with a dagger. ◆ Joan of Arc is burned as a witch.

1432 5s 3d is collected for the assize of beer at the Chagford court.

1433 A document refers to a Chapel of St Matthew at Meavy.

1434 Amongst the terms and conditions of Matilda Toker's lease on Uppaton, in Bickleigh, she is to perform suit of service to the Horrabridge courts, and also provide a day's labour every year for harrowing on the lord of the manor's (the Abbot of Buckland's) land, and another day harvesting.

1435 Richard Myleton issues a deed of homage to the Prior of Plympton, for lands in Meavy held in return for military service.

1436 Rev John Hay is murdered by Thomas Weke and others at South Brent Church.

1437 John Hulle of Harston leases Traylesworthy (Trowlesworthy) to John Nicholl jnr, the rent being set at 30s (£1 10s) a year.

1438 A contemporary document records that in this year a "great pestilence" sweeps through the city of Exeter. ◆ The 600th anniversary of the Battle of Hingston Down, where Egbert defeated the Danes and their Cornish allies.

1439 A 2lb loaf of bread costs about a farthing, as does a pint of ale. A labourer earns about 4d (approx 1½p) a week.

1440 Eton College is founded by the king. The college was later granted some land in Ugborough, which it still owned at least as late as the 1840s.

1441 Thomas Courtenay, Earl of Devon, becomes Lord Warden of the Cornish Stannaries. ◆ The Foresters' accounts record fines totalling 8s 3d received from 33 people brought before the Lydford court this year for tresspassing on the Forest with their cattle.

1442 John Jeffery is summoned to answer to the king for an encroachment on the moor between Badeworth (Batworthy) and

Mangersford and appropriating 40 acres of land for his own use.

1443 John Cheyney is appointed Sheriff of Devon. ◆ John Fortescue is Chief Justice of England.

1444 Newelcombe Tinwork, in the Newleycombe Valley, is leased to John Selman for 21 years at a rent of 6s 8d p.a.

Tin streamworks in the Newleycombe Valley (q.v. 1444).

1445 The ancient Forest Laws dictated that tenants should depasture their herds and flocks in the Forest only by day, and were to "goo home by sonne" (sundown), and in this year 52 men are fined 3d each by the Lydford manor court for staying overnight in the Forest with their beasts. At the same court, John Simon and John Holway are charged with illegally burning a large tract of pastureland near Eylesbarrow. ◆ At the manor court of Buckland Monachorum, John Smerdon, Thomas Lakeman, Sybil Meyer and others are fined for selling ale by false measures.

1446 John Trevelyan becomes Lord Warden of the Stannaries.

1447 St Eustachius Church in Tavistock is widened by the addition of what is still known as the clothworkers' aisle, with money endowed by the widow of a rich clothmaker. One of the motifs in the coat of arms of the borough of Tavistock depicts the heraldic symbol for a fleece, which can be seen in some of the windows of the church.

1448 Okehampton Church is rebuilt.

1449 James Derneford, lord of the manor of Stonehouse, is ordered to remove a pillory and tumbril which he had set up the previous year, and to pay a fine of £20 to the Abbot of Buckland for infringing on the latter's rights as lord of the Roborough hundred.

1450 The longhouse at Clannaborough is built (or perhaps rebuilt around the shell of an older building).

1451 Sir Philip Courtenay and Sir Edward Hungerford, granted the custody of the Forest in 1446 for the term of their lives, present their first set of accounts, for the previous five years, for "...the Borough of Lydford, the mill, and the courts there...the rent of the tenants of the borough...the Manor of South Teign, the mill, the courts...and of all the lands of the King called Dartmoor, and of all herbage and waste of the same lands...and all other issues and commodities...also all tenures of the Manor & Borough aforesaid...with all profits...appertaining...".

The arms of Tavistock, displayed in some of the windows in the church (q.v. 1447).

1452 The Earl of Shrewsbury, owner of estates in North Bovey and Blackadon Piper, is killed in the Battle of Castillon. His son is also killed, fighting to try and save his dying father. The estates revert to another line, until, in 1520, they come into the possession of Henry Courtenay, Earl of Devon.

1453 The Earl of Devon, "accompanied by many riotous person, as it is said, with 800 horsemen and 4,000 footmen" (as a contemporary report records), is accused of creating "great and grievous riotes in the Citie of Exon" (Exeter) and robbing the cathedral. One of many skirmishes in a long-running feud with arch-rival William Bonville, the warring culminates in the murder of Nicholas Radford two years later and the subsequent Battle of Clyst.

1454 Thomas Bourchier becomes Archbishop of Canterbury.

1455 Rebuilding of the church at Dunsford is completed.

1456 Peter Courtenay, third son of Sir Philip, leaves Moretonhampstead, where he had been rector for just three years, to first become Dean of Windsor and later Bishop of Exeter and then of Winchester, where he died in 1492. He is the only Moreton incumbent to have been ordained as a bishop.

1457 The Bailiffs' accounts of the Forest include some interesting entries in this year, recording the receipt of rent of 1½d from a tinsmith for an acre of land near Hethcote, and an identical sum from another tinsmith for an acre of land described as being "at Feyrecote next Redlake".

1458 The fee of the treasurer of the royal household for "engrossing the great account of the Duchy of Cornwall" is £1; that of the chamberlain for tallying the account of the Sheriff of Devon is 1s 8d, set fees which had been laid down by statute the previous year.

1459 The Earl of Devon openly supports the Lancastrian cause in the Wars of the Roses.

1460 Richard Westcott of Throwleigh is presented at the Lydford court for preventing the king's lieges from using the way leading to the Chapel of St Mary of Wallen and thence out into the Forest.

1461 Roger Dynham becomes Lord Warden of the Stannaries.

1462 Richard Wyke grants lands in South Tawton to Richard Northmore.

1463 Under the instigation of Philip de Coplestone, a riotous mob causes mayhem amongst the inhabitants of South Tawton, "sore bete wonded and evell entreted" a number of them and, later, "murdered and sloe" the unfortunate John Syngs. Whether the perpetrators were ever brought to justice for these crimes seems to have gone unrecorded. ◆ The manor of Belstone is granted to John Stapelhill following the beheading of Baldwin Fulford.

1464 Roborough stone is mentioned in the will of Richard Strode, who directs that a window made of "Rowburghstone" should be erected in the church at Plympton St Mary.

1465 The income of Exeter Cathedral (accounted from October 1465 to October 1466) is £1,081 7s 10d.

1466 A royal charter permits Cornish tinners to take peat from Dartmoor.

1467 The inhabitants of Tavistock (and other parishes in Devon) petition the king to relax the wool trade laws and, because of the coarseness of the local wool, permit them to mix lambs wool and flax with it. The resulting fabrics are later to become the famous Devon Serges and Tavistock White Straits.

1468 Reginald Cole and others are arraigned before the Lydford court for enclosing 200 acres of pasture on the commons of Devon between the Erme and the Yealm.

1469 John Dynham becomes Lord Warden of the Stannaries.

1470 John Berde is the tinner at Cumston, the earliest reference to tinworking at, or near, the site of the later Cumston Mine. ◆ Also in this year is found what is perhaps the earliest reference to

Cranmere Pool, named as "Cremere in Thertemore".

1471 Thomas Courtenay, Earl of Devon, who had welcomed Queen Margaret and Prince Edward when they sailed into Weymouth, is killed in the Battle of Tewkesbury after having raised an army throughout Devon and Cornwall to fight on the side of the prince. The Prince of Wales is himself also killed.

1472 About this year Sir John Fortescue writes his treatise on the governance of England.

1473 Thomas Olyver, Abbot of Buckland, is arrested for refusing to give up possession of the abbey to the newly-ordained William Breton.

1474 A Great Court of Devon Tinners is held on Crockentor, the earliest documented reference to a stannary court sitting held at this site.

1475 Chalk Ford is named in a deed as Chelkeford. Nothing to do with chalk, the name is said to mean "the ford by the [deer] calf enclosure", a not inappropriate description given the purpose to which the present-day enclosures on Scorriton Down are put.

1476 John Burghuema becomes the tenant at Stokken (Stockingtown) near Withill in Walkhampton.

1477 The earliest 'pub' on Dartmoor? – what is now the Oxenham Arms is granted its first licence to sell ale.

1478 A jury finds "agaynest the Abbot of Monkenbuclond" (Buckland Monachorum), Thomas Oliver, and dismisses his claim to sole rights of pasturage on the 10,000 or so acres of the abbey's estate on western Dartmoor (the ancient rights of Devonians to depasture livestock on the commons could not be alienated by the 1273 foundation grant of the manors to Buckland Abbey).

1479 John Houghe becomes the tenant at one of the Lowery tenements, in Walkhampton, "excepting two Closes at Lowerthy lane, formerly in the occupation of Philip Pyke"."

1480 William Bycote is fined at the Lydford manor court for stealing a horse from Huntingdon Farm the previous year.

1481 A very long-established notion (which prevailed in some places until as late as Victorian times) felt that ringing church bells could ward off thunder, and in this year William Taverner of Chagford is paid 4d by the churchwardens "for ringing when it thundered".

1482 The annual church ale held at Ashburton raises £5 13s 4d this year.

1483 John Scudamore is named in a deed as being Lord of Shittlestore (Sheepstor). It was from this family that the Elford(e)s of Yelverton inherited the lordship in 1517.

1484 Johanna Reddon grants to Thomas Ford of Comb and John Scoos of Trewyn the messuages, lands, tenements and appurtenances thereof in "Lowercatrow in the pish of Wydecomb and the tithing of Spychewyke" (Lower Cator in the tithing of Spitchwick in

Widecombe Parish).

1485 Walter Courtenay becomes Lord Warden of the Stannaries. ◆ The earliest documented reference to mineral working at a "tynworke above Wheddowne", at, or near, the site of what was later to become Whiddon Mine.

1486 Minor repairs are conducted on the church at Ashburton, requiring some new pieces of granite, and what better place to get them than Dartmoor – 5d is paid "for brede and drynke to them that cariyd stonys owte of the more", and 2s 10d (approx 14p) for "drayng [drawing, ie. hauling] stonys in the more".

1487 Thomas Foote is granted a right to build a fulling mill at Stykelpath Down, Buckland Monachorum.

1488 Thomas Dennys, John Yeo, Robert Knighton and Richard Wager are appointed arbitrators to settle a disputed right to a church way and a corpse way from Combe over Way in Chagford. ◆ Riddon is added to the list of ancient tenements of the Forest.

1489 William Ollisbrome and Thomas Harre are appointed ale tasters for the town and borough of Ashburton.

1490 John Sapcote is appointed Vice Warden of the Stannaries. ◆ The Company of Blacksmiths is founded in London; their coat of arms is to be seen on a tombstone in Mary Tavy churchyard, to Thomas Hawkins, a local blacksmith who died in 1721.

1491 The receivers of the Forest of Dartmoor record the receipt of 2d rent from Richard Canna for a parcel of land "lying between Stoddesbrook and Walbrook midstreme so descending by les midstreme of the said water called Walbrook to the Churchway of the said Richard leading from his tenement towards the Church of Widecombe".

1492 Churchwardens at Chagford raise 4s 3d from the sale of black tin from their tinworks at Bubhill.

1493 The Abbot of Buckland leases the tenement of Derkysworthy in Schyttystor (Ditsworthy in Sheepstor) to Thomas Pooell for 70 years at 13s 4d p.a., the terms of his lease including common of pasture on Rynnemore Down (Ringmoor Down) and directives to attend the courts held at Horrabridge.

1494 The Great Court of Devon Tinners meets on Crockerntor, the first meeting for which a complete transcript of the proceedings and list of jurates survives. The occasion was celebrated in a re-enactment ceremony on the tor on the 500th anniversary.

1495 £3 9s 5½d is raised at a church ale held in Chagford.

1496 John Ponsford, carpenter, is paid 3s 8d for repairing the timbers on the tower of Chagford Church; the old timbers are sold for 1s 6d (7½d).

Parliament Rock, Crockern Tor (q.v. 1494).

1497 Ashburton Church had a clock from at least as early as the 1490s, for the churchwardens' accounts record that 2s (10p) is spent on repairing it in this year. ◆ What began as a small band of Cornishmen, but by now swollen to many thousands, crosses the Tamar and passes through Tavistock en route to London, picking up many disaffected Devonians on the way. What was originally intended as a peaceful protest against the increasing tax burden is met by force at Guildford, but the king's army is routed. The Cornishmen and their followers are later defeated at the Battle of Blackheath, and their leaders hung, drawn and quartered, or beheaded.

1498 The priest of St Lawrence Chapel, Ashburton, is paid 4d for attending the mass said for Thomas Tankert.

1499 Is a document from this year the earliest reference to actual shaft mining on Dartmoor? – at, or near, the site of the later Furzehill Wood Mine, near Yelverton.

The Sixteenth Century

The magnificent rood screen in Holne Church (q.v. 1500).

1500 A rood screen is installed in Holne Church. It is said to be the finest surviving painted screen in Devon.

1501 An interesting reference in the Ashburton churchwardens' accounts proves the long held contention that places on Dartmoor with spellings such as Rowtor, Rowbrook, Crow Tor, etc, should correctly be pronounced 'Rough' Tor, 'Rough' Brook, 'Crough' Tor – in this year the wardens paid four marks "for lyme to the steppell [steeple] when he [it] was rowcaste".

1502 Robert Willoughby de Broke becomes Lord Warden of the Stannaries. ◆ The earliest reference to a smelting mill anywhere in Devon, the small blowing mill at Yellowmead, Sheepstor, appears in a deed from this year.

1503 Roger Elford, son of John of Elford Town (Yelverton), is elected Burgess of Plymouth.

1504 The earliest Baskerville?? An Edward Basker leases a cottage at Bickleigh from the Abbot of Buckland – his little dwelling could have been appropriately described as the 'Basker ville'!

1505 A Forester's account records that the "hamlett de Tenkenhmhome infra parochia de Chagford" (Teigncombe in the parish of

Chagford) pays iiijs (4s = 20p) venville rent.

1506 The Ashburton churchwardens pay 4s 5d "for pergettyng and playstryng of the mantell in Dorzed is howse and bred and ale to the playres"! Just one of many mysterious entries from the Ashburton accounts of this period, this is, in fact, a reference to a Christmas play put on by travelling performers, and the preparation of a small 'house' for the stage.

1507 New doors are fitted to John Frobber's house in Ashburton. The cost of the materials? – just 3s (15p) for the timber boards and nails!

1508 The earliest documented reference to a named tinwork anywhere in the Walkham Valley, a site at, or near, Bukter.

1509 Sir Henry Marney becomes Lord Warden of the Stannaries.

1510 A new law is passed which permits any man to dig for tin anywhere within the county of Devon. This was superseded by an Act of 1574 which limited explorations to certain types of land although, rather oddly, agricultural land was still not excluded. ◆ The Prior of Plympton is accused of illegally taking water out of the Dean Burn at Tynneren Mead.

1511 Thomas Predyaux becomes senior churchwarden at St Andrew's, Ashburton.

1512 John Thomas Coole and others are charged that they "unlawfully and riotously, in the manner of an insurrection, entered and broke into the liberty of the Lord the King of his Manor of Lydford, and riotously took and drove away forty oxen and steers, and ten geldings, of the goods and chattels of the said John Coole, taken by the Bailiff".

1513 Johanne Splott and Matilda Hole are wardens of one of the guilds attached to Chagford Church this year. Although female churchwardens served elsewhere at this very early period (eg, Ashburton), this was a fairly rare occurrence, and Chagford is the only place where two women have been found serving together in the same year (which actually occurred on a number of occasions in this parish). Conversely, the first woman churchwarden at Ugborough did not serve until over four centuries later! Her headstone stands in the graveyard there.

1514 John Bourchier lets an acre of land in the manor of Spechewyke (Spitchwick) and also "a myll there called a blowyng myll and knackyng myll" to Christopher Prous and Richard Hamlyn.

1515 John Elford becomes lord of the manor and free hamlet of Sheepstor upon the death of the last of the Scudamores, lords of the manor since c1390.

1516 A lease provides evidence of the origins of the rather odd name of

The ruins of Longstone, seat of the lords of the manor of Sheepstor, during the remedial and consolidation work undertaken in 1998 (q.v. 1515).

the property in Sheepstor called Scotland, Roger Elleford granting to Nicholas Liteltor "a tenement in Chubbeston and a piece of land in Stocland, with common of pasture upon Shipstor" – presumably the land in question was originally a small area for keeping livestock.

1517 John Odymer, son of William, takes a lease on a tenement at Hachenhylle (Hatshill) in Bickleigh for a term of 70 years at 17s (85p) p.a. – the rent is the same as it had been in 1458. The next surviving lease is not until three centuries later, 1758, by which time the rent had increased to 30s (£1.50p) p.a.

1518 Richard Strode, MP for Plympton, is imprisoned in "one of the most heinous, contagious, and detestable places within the realm" for three weeks, an event which later gives rise to the convention known as parliamentary privilege; the place described is the dungeon at Lydford Castle.

1519 A riotous assembly meets at Horrabridge, armed with "crosebowes & quarells bowes & arrowes swords bokelers bills & stavys & other wepons", and descends on the Furzehill tinwork intent on stealing some tin.

1520 No Ashburtonian requires the bells to be rung at any funerals this year, so the churchwarden does not need to pay the bellringers for performing this duty. However, he still decides to make an entry to this effect in his accounts, recording a payment of "nothing for ringing at no-one's obit"!

1521 Another two ancient tenements are added to the growing list, those of Prince Hall and Herterlande (Hartiland).

1522 Richard Hamlyn of Widecombe pays the lay subsidy for his ownership of Chittleford, Scobetor, Venton, Dunstone and Blackslade (all in Widecombe), and Dawnton (in Buckfastleigh).

1523 Henry Courtenay, Marquis of Exeter, becomes Lord Warden of the Stannaries.

1524 Earliest mention of Bubhill tinwork, on a tiny scrap of parchment which records that it is let to a William Vyse or Veysey.

1525 A printing press is established in Tavistock (in the Benedictine abbey), only the fifth town in England to have one. A book entitled *Here folyth the Confirmation of the Charter perteynynge to all the tynners wythyn the Countey of Deuonshyre, with there Stututes also made at Crockeryntorre by the hole Assent & Csent of al the sayd tynners Yn the yere of the reygne of our souerayngе Lord Kynge Henry viij, the secund yere* is one of only two books printed there which still survive.

1526 Robert Hoare of Chagford bequeaths 6 marks towards the repainting of the rood loft in the church (1 mark = 13s 4d = approx 66p).

1527 Richard Latymer grants the "blowyng tynmyll" at Blackaller, North Bovey, to Richard Wavell of Moreton. ◆ John Kelly, lord of the manor of Kelly, arming himself with a pair of pistols, leads a riotous mob of some 300 local farmers and peasants to Gulworthy, on the River Tamar, intent on destroying the fishing weir there (this had recently been erected by the monks of Tavistock Abbey, to the detriment of the fishermen higher upstream). As they are dismantling and burning the weir, they espy a throng of 160 men of Tavistock, armed with cudgels, mattocks and other weapons, marching out to meet them – led by the Abbot of Tavistock himself!

1528 John Tucker of Moreton becomes the last Abbot of Buckland. At the dissolution he surrendered the abbey to Henry VIII and was forced to retire on a pension of £60 p.a. (which, by the way, he did receive – he was still alive in 1555, and drawing his pension).

1529 The sum given for St Peter's Pence (also known as Romescot) by South Tawton is 2s; Chagford pays 13½d. Other Dartmoor parishes also make their fixed annual contributions to this levy, which was soon to be transferred from the papacy to the Crown (following the Act of Supremacy in 1534).

1530 Richard Turpyn of Ashburton is paid 6s 8d "as a reward from the parishioners for his assistance in singing" in the church.

1531 The coinage rolls for Tavistock mention "St Dionisius of

Walkynton". This document was only rediscovered very recently, and the original dedication of the church at Walkhampton had until then been unknown – in 1985 it was rededicated to St Mary the Virgin.

1532 Sir Philip Champernown is appointed Vice Warden of the Stannaries.

1533 An Act "To dystroye Choughes, Crowes and Rokes" (superseded in 1566 by the Act against "Noyfull Fowles & Vermyn") authorises churchwardens in Dartmoor parishes (and in rural parishes throughout the nation) to pay monetary rewards for the killing of creatures perceived as 'vermin'.

1534 "2 kyves, 2 costs, a barrel, 2 gyrdilles harnysed with sylver, 16 barres of sylver, a charger, 4 platters, a potynger, a saucer, 4 sylver rings, the chythe, 4 lawn kerchers" – these are the items listed in an inventory of the stock of the store of St Katheryne's, a guild belonging to Chagford Church. How many of them survived the upheavals which were to follow? Or did they all end up in the king's 'melting pot'?

1535 The rent of 8d is paid to the Ashburton reeve by the (unnamed) occupier of "serten growne and the tenement of Pottekesland" (certain ground and the tenement at Puttesham; now Lower Pudsham).

1536 The Valor Ecclesiastica values Widecombe Church and glebe at £10 10s p.a. ◆ South Tawton parishioners contribute £3 9s 4d to the 'Fifty Dole', a royal tax representing a fifteenth of the nominal value of properties within the parish.

1537 A year before Gabriel Dunne finally surrenders Buckfast Abbey, Henry VIII appropriates part of its holdings and leases the tithes and sheaf of hay of Brent to John Southcote and Anthony Burleigh for 60 years at £20 p.a.

1538 Adam Williams is appointed under-steward of the Ashburton Stannary.

1539 Sir John Russell becomes Lord Warden of the Stannaries.

1540 The monastic holding of Sweaton Farm "in Specheweke" (Spitchwick) is granted to John Southcott of Bovey Tracey.

1541 The Chagford churchwardens pay 26s 9d to William Honywyll for his labour working at Bubhill tinwork during the Rodemas Wash.

1542 Lewis Fortescue and others are assigned to "inquire and make a survey of the limits, metes, and bounds of the lord the Prince's Forest of Dartmoor and the commons and wastes of the said Forest". No survey report survives but a recital of the customs and rights of the Forest is thought to date from this year (earlier documents recording the laws of the Forest also survive). ◆ John

Langadon is one of the shareholders of a tinwork at "Welaby above Dry Lakes" on the O Brook.

1543 George Ford is reeve of the borough of Ashburton.

1544 Richard Langworthy of Litzwill buys Ponsworthy Mill from John Bourchier.

1545 The value of the ornaments, jewels, plate, goods and chattels belonging to the guild of St Lawrence, Ashburton is "xxxviijli ixs iiid [£38 9s 3d] and besydes dyv'se sylv' rynges wt other certayne jewelles and ornamentes of small pryce wch are not here valued".

1546 The manor of Walkhampton is bought by John Slanning of Plympton. ◆ In this year there are just eight registered taxpayers living in Belstone Parish, paying sums varying from between 3s 4d (approx 17p) and 12s (60p) each.

1547 The Ashburton churchwardens contribute 10s (50p) towards the costs of "repairing the bryge called Dart brygge". Under the decrees laid down by the king's injunctions, they also have to order the forfeiture of most of the ornaments and jewels belonging to their church. Much of the interior is also ravaged, and the rood screen and altar are destroyed.

1548 Edward Seymour, Duke of Somerset, becomes Lord Warden of the Stannaries.

1549 The Battle of Fenny Bridges brings an end to the Western Rebellion.

1550 John, Lord Russell, who had purchased most of the estate of Tavistock Abbey after the dissolution, is created the Earl of Bedford. The estate was to become a dukedom in 1694.

1551 Richard Strode of Newnham and Plympton dies. His inquisition post mortem of the following year records that the Dartmoor properties owned by the family comprise – 2s rent in Cadworthy, Meavy; a messuage etc, 40 acres of land etc at Legh, Ugborough, held of Thomas Wyllyams; a messuage etc, 40 acres of land etc at Lovaton, Meavy, held of the heirs of Bastard Bonvyle; a messuage etc, 40 acres of woodland at Myllond, Shaugh; 100 acres of brake, 8 acres of wood at Shadon and Northwode, Shaugh, held of John Slanning; a messuage etc at Cuttorston, Shaugh, held of Nicholas Cole; and, rather surprisingly, six messuages etc in the borough of Ashburton, held of Miles, Bishop of Exeter. Lands and properties around Newnham and elsewhere are also listed in the deed.

1552 John Whiddon of Chagford becomes a judge of the King's Bench and is knighted the following year: he was to serve as a judge until he died in 1575. ◆ John Russell, Earl of Bedford, becomes Lord Warden of the Stannaries.

1553 George Mylford makes a complaint in the manor court at South

Tawton against John Wykes, parish constable, that he did "bete wounde and evell entrete" him, so that he was "in dispere of his lyef", and also did "dryve and chase wt dogges" a hundred of his ewes. ◆ Ellys Sholabear of Sheepstor is the cowherd in charge of the Strode-owned cattle depastured on Dartmoor. In this year he is paid 12d for this duty, which sum also includes the payment for the venville rent.

1554 Edward Courtenay, imprisoned in the Tower by Edward VI, is released by Mary, who later bestows on him the title of Earl of Devon. ◆ Fortune does not smile so well on Dr John Rogers, who is imprisoned, and is burnt at the stake the following year. One of his descendants, also John, bought the Blachford Estate in 1694.

1555 Sir Edward Hastings becomes Lord Warden of the Stannaries. ◆ Harford Church is today always known as St Petroc's, and has been for an unknown period of time. However, a deed from this year describes it as being dedicated to St George the Martyr.

Harford Church – St Petroc's or St George's? (q.v. 1555).

1556 Phylyp Brockedon of Kyngsbrygge, merchant, sells the messuage and tenement at Chapple in Taynton Drewe (Drewsteignton) to Thomas Noseworthy of Maneton, taylor, for £15. ◆ South Tawton spends 16d on furze for the fire beacon atop Cosdon.

1557 An inquisition is held into the bounds of Brent Moor, and four crosses are set up to mark its limits (of which only Huntingdon Cross survives intact; the mutilated shaft of Petre's Cross is to be seen on Western Whittaburrow).

1558 Church bells across the nation ring out announcing the death of Queen Mary. At Ashburton the ringers are paid 8d for "ryngyng of Quenez Mary ys knyll", as the churchwardens' accounts record.

1559 After having expended large sums of money in repairing the damage done to their church during the reign of Henry VI (q.v. 1547) and restored the interior to something akin to its former glory, the whole process is repeated again, and the Ashburton churchwardens have to spend 10d "for ther [their] labor that carryed the Images to be burnt, and the drynkyng".

1560 Willmo Mayow pays John Strode 5d for "pastur yn le wasts of Shagh" (pasturing rights on the wastes in Shaugh Prior). Meanwhile, John Mayow, "moreman", is paid 10s by Strode for "comen on my wasts thys yere".

1561 The South Tawton churchwardens record the payment of £1 to the vicar "to help pay his subsidye and tenth unto the queyns maiestie" (a reference to the payment of first-fruits and tenths, paid annually to the Crown since the break with Rome).

1562 Thomas Noseworthe of Maneton buys a close of land called Brendon, part of the manor of Moreton, from George Selake of Dawlysshe for £29. The present occupiers are George and Thomas Grey. ◆ Philip Cole of Slade Manor leases to James More the tenement and farm of Wisdome in Cornwood, plus closes of land at Hele Park, with common of pasture on Staldon and Hanger Down.

1563 Thomas Williams of Stowford becomes Speaker of the House of Commons. He died three years later and is buried in Harford Church, where a pair of brass memorial plaques bear an appropriate inscription. ◆ The head churchwarden at South Tawton is excommunicated because "the rode lofte was not taken down". ◆ Bremberry becomes the last of the ancient tenements of the Forest to be documented. Hardly 'ancient' in the true sense of the word, for the earliest references to Babeny and Pizwell predate it by at least three centuries (q.v. 1260) (these latter two have also outlived it, for the dwelling house at what was later called Brownberry is now a total ruin).

1564 Andrew Bonsall of Shyttistor (Sheepstor) buys tenements at Combeshead in Harford, Pithill in Cornwood and lands in Horrabridge and Sampford Spiney from Thomas Walk of Tavystocke (Tavistock). The cost is just 20 marks (which was the equivalent of £13 6s 8d = £13.33p).

1565 Chagford market wardens, John Bonymay and Robert Haydon, pay the market clerk for "seyllyng of Market Whyetts" (sealing – ie. stamping – of the market weights). This function needed to be performed annually, the weights and measures used at all markets being checked and approved by the clerks.

1566 Thomas Williams, in his will, aside from leaving his wife the Stowford Estate and all lands in Harford etc, also bequeaths "a meyde to weyte on her, meate and drinke in the mansion house of Stowford, and a Nagge with sufficient grass in some and in winter, and a man and horse to goo & ryde withe her".

1567 Sir Nicholas Slanning lays claim to the whole of Walkhampton Commons as his exclusive right. In a re-run of an earlier case on exactly the same contentious issue (q.v. 1478) judgement is given against him. ◆ George Ford sells Nether Grevetors and other lands in Manaton to John Hole and John Bowle.

1568 John Fitz, after having become lost on the moor, erects a small chamber over a well near Princetown, whose waters, he claims, broke the pixies' spell which had caused him to stray off his route. The well is today still known as Fice's Well, and the dated lintel erected by Fitz is still in place.

Fice's Well, near Princetown (q.v. 1568).

1569 Peter Woodley purchases Halsanger Manor from George Ford. ◆ 1,583 cattle are driven up onto the western quarter of the moor for summer pasturage. The largest herd, 200 head of cattle, is sent by William Edmund; Gregory Man sends just one beast. The agistment fees are $1^{1}/_{4}$d per head for the five months from June to October.

1570 John Elford conveys a building (later to become the church house) "forever in Trust for the whole Parish of Sheepstor". ◆ Christopher Sumpter pays 2s 6d p.a. rent for a "tokyng myll" (tucking, or fulling, mill) in Shaugh Prior.

1571 Hugh Littletor is the farmer at Combshead, Sheepstor. Presumably the personal name is also seen in the later Litteltors Worke Pitt, a tinwork at nearby Outcombe. ◆ Bartholomew Pope becomes the seneschalle (steward) of the Strode Estates, which include lands and property in Meavy and Shaugh.

1572 John Weekes ('Warrior Weekes') of North Wyke is named as being a "Captayne of the Posse Comitatus" (County Militia). ◆ Francis Russell, Earl of Bedford, becomes Lord Warden of the Stannaries. ◆ Bartholomew Gidlegh is constable of the borough of Sele (South Zeal).

1573 John and Maria Creston become the tenants at West Loworthie (Lowery) in Walkhampton Parish, paying a yearly rent of 10s 6d. Their neighbours at East Loworthie are Johes and Johan (John and Joan) Shulabere, who have been there since 1562, paying 8s 2d p.a. ◆ Laurens Edmunds Rowe, "Reve of the fforest of dartemore", spends 13s 4d on "mending the walles and making of a new yate [gate]" at Donabrydge (Dunnabridge) Pound.

1574 Harrye Couke of Ashburton is paid £1 "for setting fourth of souldyers to serve the Quenes majestie" at a muster call of soldiers of the hundred.

1575 Sir John Whiddon, a judge of the King's Bench at Westminster, dies. He is buried at Chagford.

1576 The Duchy court, held in Lydford, grants John Williams of Harford the right to graze pigs in the Forest. ◆ The churchwardens of Dean Prior forfeit 5s (25p) on behalf of their parishioners for the latter disobeying the Act stipulating that everyone had to wear a woollen hat "on sondaies and holy daies" (passed in 1570 in order to help the wool trade).

1577 William Hellier becomes vicar of Bickleigh and Sheepstor under the patronage of Sir Nicholas Slannynge.

1578 John Prideaux, later to become Bishop of Worcestor, is born at Stowford, described in his epitaph (in Bredon Church, Worcs) as "an obscure place in Devonshire". Indeed, Stowford , in Harford Parish, is so "obscure" that the birthplace of John Prideaux has often been mistakenly recorded as having been the *parish* of Stowford, near the Cornish border.

1579 The court at Lydford gives Richard Ellacott just one day to effect repairs to Sowtherly Gate, opening upon the Forest, under penalty of a fine of 10s (50p) for failing to do so. The court, held the following year, records that the offending gate had, indeed, been repaired.

1580 A minor earthquake rocks parts of Dartmoor. Later in the year the churchwardens at Chagford pay 10d "for a book of prayer upon the Earthquake". ◆ A document refers to lodestone, or magnetite, mining on Brent Hill. The exact location of the works is unknown.

1581 Buckland Abbey, owned by the Grenvilles since the dissolution, is bought by Sir Francis Drake.

1582 The tithe payments at Meavy are 1d for every milkable cow, ½d for every calf, 1d for every colt, ¼d for every lamb, pig and goose, ¼d for a wool fleece, ¼d for a milking ewe, 1d for each garden plot, 10th of every hogshead of apples and 2d for every hogshead of cider; all to be paid at the Feast of Easter; oxen employed for tillage are exempt.

1583 John Ellet and Robert French are each amerced 6d in the Lydford court for not carrying out the drift in the eastern quarter of the Forest.

1584 Sir Walter Raleigh becomes Lord Warden of the Stannaries. ◆ A total of £1 16s is collected for the venville rents for the south quarter of the Forest. The lowest sum is paid by Ugborough, its inhabitants paying just 5d (approx 2p) for their rights; Holne, on the other hand, pays 18s (90p).

1585 "An acte for the presvacon of the Haven of Plymouth" orders the cutting of a "Dytche or Trenche conteynenge in breadthe betwene sixe or seaven Foote...betweene the saide Towne...and any parte of the saide Ryver of Mewe" to bring water to the town, which it states is a "thing verey necessarie". This is to become known as the Plymouth, or Drake's, Leat.

1586 John Ford, the dramatist, is born in Ilsington.

1587 For the better protection and maintenance of "ye natyve pore people", the parishioners of Ugborough are ordered to "Remove and dysplace Everye Suche person Lyklye to burden or charge this parish" who had not been born in the parish. The order, signed by around 80 parishioners, is the more remarkable for it actually predates the Act of Settlement.

1588 Sir Nicholas Slanning and his tenants, accompanied by the lords of the adjoining manors, view the bounds of Shaugh Manor on Ascension Day.

1589 The inhabitants of Brisworthy are once again presented for failing to repair the harte yeate opening upon the commons, in a long-running dispute which had begun in 1582. Despite numerous similar presentments, and fines being imposed, it appears that the gate had still not been repaired as late as 1608.

1590 William Browne, the poet, is born in Tavistock.

1591 Robert Herrick, later to become vicar of Dean, and poet, is born in London, the son of a family of goldsmiths. ◆ Plymouth, or Drake's, Leat brings water from the moor to Plymouth for the first time.

1592 Fifty people are buried in three months at Bovey (triple the normal death toll), most of them probably falling victim to the flu epidemic which is sweeping the nation.

1593 Raphe Woodleigh of Buckland-in-the-Moor, "Gentleman Lord of this Mannour" (as his tombstone records), dies and is interred in St Peter's Church, Buckland. His tombstone is the oldest dated ledger which has survived in any of the churches on Dartmoor. ◆ Humphrey Tylham of Cornwood conveys his moiety of a tinworks called "Readaclyffe streaming to Langabrydge" in Cornwood to William Sherwill the elder, tinner of Cornwood.

1594 Cornelius Jansen paints a portrait of Sir Francis Drake of Buckland Abbey.

1595 195 pieces of tin, weighing a total of 31,160lbs, are coined at Tavistock.

1596 A certain part of Thomas Smerdon's anatomy is mentioned in a Bovey Tracey rate list – "Thomas Smerdon for his House and Backside 2d"! The entry, of course, refers to the rear courtyard adjoining the property.

1597 General Gorges inspects "two hundred men from Erme & Plympton under Mr Seymour, three companies of tinners, and all the horse of the district" during a muster of volunteer forces on Roborough Down.

1598 Researchers normally expect to find that modern placenames are simpler corruptions of rather more obscure former names, but on occasions it seems that the opposite is the case. In this year Hugh Elforde sells Southtowne in Peter Tavy to Robert Moore. It is appropriately named for, aside from a couple of isolated farms just to the south, the place is the most southerly 'town', or settlement/hamlet, in the parish. But the farmstead is today known as Sowtontown, the 'town' element in the placename having been duplicated.

1599 Philip Strode buys Thomas Deane's shares in the tinworks at Greate Willings, Middle Plyme, Hynterbrooke and Weallabrooke.

*****

The Seventeenth Century

1600 The Buckland Monachorum waywardens spend the princely sum of 15s 4d (approx $76^1/_2$p) on their roads this year!

1601 John Woollcombe and Richard Hele pitch the bounds of a tinwork "lying upon ye very Ridge of the hill above Hentor Hill Shabbercombe and Colemore ridge streaming towards yealme".

1602 Amongst the possessions listed in the inquisition post mortem of John Hunt of Bickleigh are a "fowling peece, a crossbow, a bow and six arrowes". ◆ William George and William Stephens, millers, are presented at the Buckland Monachorum manor court for charging excessive prices.

1603 William Herbert, Earl of Pembroke, becomes Lord Warden of the Stannaries.

1604 Whilst Shakespeare is putting the final touches to his *Hamlet*, Sir Walter Raleigh is beginning his second year of imprisonment in the Tower of London for treason.

1605 Lord Pembroke writes to the justices of the King's Bench and the Court of Common Pleas requesting them to refrain from hearing cases which ought to be tried by the stannary courts, thereby causing unnecessary expense and inconvenience to poor tinners having to travel to London to answer to "frivolous charges".

1606 Andrew Cholwyche of Cholwyche[town] agrees to buy the manor of Down Thomas from Thomas Maynard for £500, but for some unknown reason the sale is not carried through.

1607 John Hext is the postmaster at the Ashburton staging post (for post riders). His wages are 2s per day.

1608 The church house at Widecombe is leased to John Baker for £2 p.a. with a provision that he allows the parishioners to hold a church ale in the house "once or twice a yere and use the said house and butt park att convenient tymes as they have bin accustomed". ◆ John Hannaford pays 3d for the lease of Wikeford Milles and two acres of land at Week Ford.

1609 Another perambulation of the bounds of the Forest of Dartmoor is held.

1610 William Hunt, rector of Lydford, files a suit against the parishioners of Whitchurch and Tavistock for the tithe of the agistment of sheep in the Forest, in the first of a long-running series of disputes over tithes between the commoners and various rectors of Lydford.

1611 Following on from this, Gregory Newman, vicar of Walkhampton, is charged with appropriating tithe payments which Hunt believes belong to him. And so the story continues, off and on, for nigh on a century or more, successive Lydford rectors bringing various suits from time to time.

1612 John Nosworthy, who was to become the first to preach on the (later) site of the Ashburton Great Meeting House (Independent Church), is born in Manaton.

1613 Richard Reynell and Walter Fursland lease from William Bourchier, Earl of Bath, an extensive area of Spitchwick Common between Heartor, Cornetor, Rowbrook Hedge and the River of Darte, with free liberty "for the keeping breeding and killing of rabbits", forming what was later to become known as Vaghill Warren. Robert Meade, Richard Reynell's warrener who was killed in the Great Storm of 1638, probably worked at Vaghill at the time.

1614 Richard Cole of Slade dies and is buried at Cornwood, the family coat of arms surmounting his memorial in the church. Richard's great x5 grandfather, Sir John Cole, carried them into battle at Agincourt in 1415. They are one of only two coats of arms borne at the battle which may be seen in any of the Dartmoor churches (the other is at Drewsteignton, q.v. 1415).

1615 The Hawne tenement in Cornwood is leased by William Strode to Solomon Andrew at a rent of £1 6s 8d p.a. Included in the terms and conditions are common rights for the tenants to depasture "all theyr beasts and cattell upon the moore there called pennymoore" (Pen Moor).

1616 Wadham College in Oxford is completed at a cost of £10,816. It takes its name from the family who owned Lustleigh Manor (q.v. 1414), the college having been founded (or, more correctly perhaps, proposed) by Nicholas Wadham, last of the line. Although he died in 1609 before his wishes could be put into effect, they were eventually carried out by his widow.

1617 A most curious way of describing the unfortunate demise of Gabriel Aptor appears in the Widecombe burial register, which states that he was "spoyled in a tin worke"!

1618 The chamber in which a stannary court sitting is being held in Chagford collapses under the weight of "a greater Concourse of People than ordinary...the Timber yielding, the walls fell in and slew the Steward".

1619 Richard Foster becomes Francis Courtenay's tenant at Higher, or Middle, Rooke in Cornwood at a rent of £1 8s p.a.

1620 One of the Heles of Cornwood owns a half share of a tinwork called Great Drusslecombe and a third part of Lower Drusslecombe in the Thrushelcombe Valley, at the site of the later Eylesbarrow Mine. The following year Alice Hele of Cornwood, widow, conveys these shares, along with a third share of Higher Headon, plus a half share in the tinworks at Lower Headon, to Walter Hele.

1621 Littlecombe in Holne (where the riding stables are today) is owned by Christopher Hamlyn.

1622 Lydia Mill, formerly a fulling mill, is now a grist mill; in a much later era it will become a wheelwright's shop and forge.

1623 New bounds are pitched on the Keaglesburrowe Sett "lieing between Clasawell and Reedapitt Beame". The sett is owned by John Woollcombe and Walter Elford. ◆ A meteorite falls near Sir George Chudleigh's house at Stretchleigh.

1624 Francis Whiddon becomes rector of Moretonhampstead, where he was to remain throughout the reign of Charles I and the civil war until he died there in 1656. His memorial is to be seen in the nave of the church, and is known to locals as the 'Watchman's Tomb' on account of the words in one of the verses of the epitaph.

1625 523 people die of the plague in Tavistock.

1626 Charles I grants a lease on the Forest of Dartmoor to Sir Thomas Reynell for 31 years at a rent of £28 12s 5d p.a., but Reynell does not hold it for his full term (q.v. 1634). ◆ A typhus epidemic hits

Ringmoor Down Copse, planted in the early 19th century at Portlane Head, the starting point for early beatings of the bounds of Sheepstor Manor (q.v. 1626).

Ashburton – the death toll rockets to ten times the normal annual average. ◆ Amongst the "ancient persons" of Sheepstor – the senior citizens of the parish – who (with others) beat the bounds of the free manor and hamlet of Sheepstor are Richard and John Woollacombe, Richard Bounsall, Barnard Elford, Walter Dunderidge, Stephen Knight and Charles Stuttaford.

1627 In a deposition in a tithe suit, William Torre of Widecombe describes the Forest thus – "A great part of the Forest of Dartmoor is a barren, hilly place, and dangerous to be passed through in winter by reason of mires, waters and rocks".

1628 Arthur Smerdon leases the messuage and tenements etc at "Tonehill alias Tunhill" to his brother Edward (the deed bears the signature of Edward who, interestingly, spells his surname Smeardon).

1629 Horrabridge (the ancient bridge itself) is repaired.

The Horra Bridge on the River Walkham (q.v. 1629).

1630 Philip Herbert, Earl of Pembroke and Montgomery, becomes Lord Warden of the Stannaries. ◆ Westcote visits Gidleigh, but has no particular desire to "make longer stay in this coarse place than we willingly would"!

1631 A household inventory of John Stangcombe of Ilsington records that he died possessed of, amongst other things, "one sylver spoone (value 6s), a cauldron and two skillets (9s), two packe saddles with crookes gurses lyme pottes donge pottes and a corn pike (17s), two flitches of bacon and a scrubb of beefe (15s), furse faggots (40s), sewle and seede (40s), one journey of corne in the earth (20s), his beasts and cattells (£19), plowstuffe (8s), and one little pigge (4s)".

1632 Three bells are cast for Widecombe Church by Thomas Pennington of Exeter. ◆ Sir Thomas Reynell brings a suit against owners for depasturing large numbers of sheep, cattle and colts on the moor throughout the year but taking them off before the drifts, thus defrauding him of his fees. ◆ James Howel writes of a "strange thing" which he saw in a monumental mason's shop near Fleet St, London, a large stone upon which was inscribed epitaphs to a number of Oxenhams, which included the lines: "Here lies Elizabeth Oxenham, the Mother of the said John, who died sixteen years since, when such a bird with a white breast was seen about her bed before her Death". The epitaph to John also apparently mentions the bird, and the final words on the stone record that it is destined "for a town hard by Exeter where this happen'd". There is, however, a major discrepancy with respect to the dating of this report, the full recital of which is also more unbelievable than the legend itself, and it is undoubtedly purely fictitious (q.v. 1635).

1633 Walter Elford rebuilds Longstone Manor, Sheepstor. ◆ John Farren of Peter Tavy, along with many other Devonians, emigrates to Australia.

1634 Sir Thomas Reynell reassigns his lease on the Forest of Dartmoor (q.v. 1626) to Sir Nicholas Slanning. The civil war interrupts his period of tenure (he is killed during the campaign), and the manor of Lydford and the Forest reverts to Parliament (who actually sell it!) (q.v. 1650).

1635 Sir Nicholas Slanning, and others, enquire into the state of the harbour of Plymouth, and find that its silting-up is being "occasioned by the great quantity of sand and earth which dyvers tynners working in a Tynneworke called Clasiewell and other works and Tynne Mills...which fall into the said harbour out of the said workes and Mylles". ◆ John Selman of Newton Abbot sells tenements at Higher Catrewe (Cator) to Edward Goulde of Staverton for £190. ◆ Perhaps even more strange than the legend of the 'White Bird of the Oxenhams' is the fact that the tombstone to John Oxenham was supposedly seen three years before he died!! (if later reports on the incident are to be believed – q.v. 1632). The legend has its origins in this year, when a white bird is seen hovering above the bed of John – two days later he is dead (his burial is recorded in the South Tawton register, thereby providing absolute proof of the date of the event). The most recent visitation of the ill omen apparently took place in 1919.

PRotectors, Parliaments, and all, see, hear,
And quake for fear : O do not jeer, nor swear
'Gainst God, who roars from Sion on your sin,
'Gainst such High-places which you worship in.
Jah with his burning blasts of lightnings quells
The Peoples Idols—Temples—Steeples—Bells.

A most prodigious & fearefull storme of winde lightning & thunder, mightily defacing Withcomb-ch--urch in Deuon, burneing and slayeing diverse men and women all this in service-time, on the Lords day Octob: 21-1638.

A page from a contemporary pamphlet on the Great Storm, printed in London just three weeks after the event (q.v. 1638).

1636 George Lyde becomes vicar of Widecombe. It was he who was conducting the service when a violent storm struck the church two years later.

1637 The parishioners of Ilsington donate £2 10s 6d towards the rebuilding of "the famous Cathedral Church of St Paul's in London". ◆ John Windyatt, blacksmith, leases from Thomas Williams "all those two houses...adjoining to the Mills called Ivybridge Mills...all that one other house there called the Shopp...all that one house in which the Edgemill there now is...which are adjoining to the Mill there commonly called the Malt Mill". The site is that which was in recent years known as Glanville's Mill, demolished in the 1970s to make way for the Ivybridge Shopping Centre. ◆ Henry Osborne is tried at Exeter Castle for tresspassing on Staldon Moor.

1638 The Great Storm wreaks havoc at Widecombe, destroying the tower of the church there and killing or wounding a number of the congregation.

1639 The original lych gate at Ilsington is destroyed when a woman passes under it and lets the gate swing back too heavily, dislodging a stone from the supporting wall which, in turn, brings the entire structure tumbling to the ground. Remarkably, not one of the fifteen or so children who, at the time, are being taught in the little schoolroom above the gate is seriously injured in the

The lych gate at Ilsington Church, rebuilt after the original was destroyed (q.v. 1639).

accident. ◆ Ellis Giles of Walkhampton is brought before Humfry Prouz, JP, for sheepstealing. ◆ Anne Hill of Widecombe, whose husband was killed in the Great Storm the previous year, grants the property of Woode in Widecombe to her son Richard.

1640 Henry Smith, recently appointed vicar of Cornwood, is "treated in a most barbarous and inhuman manner [and] sent to a Common Jayl in Exceter". He dies there shortly afterwards, his estate is sequestrated, and Walter Shute is appointed as the new vicar by the Puritans (q.v. 1649). ◆ Robert Herrick publishes his volume of poems entitled *Hesperides*. He is also soon to be ousted from his incumbency at Dean, but later returned (q.v. 1648).

1641 Mary Whiddon is shot by a jealous former lover as she leaves Chagford Church following her wedding. Her tombstone can be seen in the church (or not, as the case may be – the ledger is in the chancel and the rood screen doors are presently padlocked shut, so visitors cannot see the stone itself).

1642 Robert Burgoyne pays 12s (60p) tax on his property in Belstone, the second highest payment by any of the Belstone parishioners. He is likely to be the same person whose initials appear on a large mural to a number of members of the Burgoyne family, which was erected in neighbouring South Tawton Church in 1651, where it may still be seen to this day.

1643 The Battle of Chagford, between parliamentarians and royalists, is fought on the hills around Wonson and Providence Place. A cross head which sits atop a wall opposite Blackaton House is said to have been originally erected as a memorial to those killed in the fighting. ◆ Later this same year five Cornish royalist regiments, comprising 300 dragoons, 300 horses and 3,000 foot soldiers, are put to flight on Sourton Down by just 108 parliamentarian cavalrymen in the first of a series of engagements in this area of Devon.

1644 William Browne writes of *Lydford Law*.

1645 £13 is earmarked for the repair of New Bridge on the River Dart.

1646 Following the death, in 1641, of Mary Gale, his third wife, John Elford marries for a fourth time, to Sarah Woolcombe, by whom he has seven sons – to add to the eleven children he had fathered by his previous three marriages (not all of the children, by any of his marriages, survived their infancy, so the family was never an enormously large one).

1647 The farm at Higher Bremley, Ilsington, is split into four holdings. John Bowden's quarter share comprises "all the Barn and Linnies under the same roof, the Barn Garden, Barn Courtlage, four of the best trees in the Moore and Moore Head, and the fields called

Laye, Lower Downe, the lower end of Higher Downe, and Queen Parks". Richard Lyell owns another quarter part of the farm, Edward Furlong the remaining half. ◆ Thomas Harragrove sells his "Tenement in Lydford called and commonly known by the name of Wotek mill" to William Walter for £30. ◆ Christopher Bond of Ashburton, who had been bound over to appear at the Exeter assizes, is ordered not to appear "because the plague is now in Ashburton".

1648 Robert Herrick is ousted as vicar of Dean Prior. He later returned to this little patch of his beloved (?!) Devonshire, and was once more vicar of Dean from 1662 until his death in 1674.

1649 Walter Shute, described in a contemporary letter as an "ignorant and gluttonous fellow", preaches a blasphemous sermon in Cornwood Church, deriding kings and princes, after the execution of Charles I. After the Restoration he conformed (perhaps so that he would not lose his own head?!), and was granted clemency.

1650 The last execution takes place in Lydford Castle. Coincidentally, at the same time the borough of Lydford, now in the hands of Parliament, is sold to William Braddon of Stoke Climsland.

1651 The earliest definite reference to warrening at Trowlesworthy.

1652 John Shebbeare becomes Mayor of Okehampton.

1653 Bartholomew Gidley, "a man of great contrivances", diverts the Bradford Pool Leat, thus ushering in the early beginnings of another in a long-running series of disputes over water rights in the Bradford Pool/Gidleigh Commons/Throwleigh Commons area. However, it was not until 1698, ten years after the Bradford Pool tinworks (re)opened, that litigation finally ensued.

1654 Alexander Coombe conveys "a tinworke wholly mine commonly called or knowne by the name of Holwood Parke within the parish of Mewy the head thereof lyinge in Holwood warren" to Edward Maunder. ◆ John Browne of Ashburton is "buried in the High way near Gooseapoole", as the entry in the burial register records.

1655 Squire Cabell of Brook Manor dies and is incarcerated in a small mausoleum erected over a massive chest tomb in Buckfastleigh churchyard, the building said to have been erected as a precaution to prevent his evil spirit escaping (but which, in fact, actually predates his own death by a few years, having originally been erected over the graves of other members of the family).

1656 Shilstone Farm, Throwleigh, undergoes a major restoration and rebuild.

1657 Humphrey Waldron, banished to Spain in 1650, becomes a marquis and grandee. This branch of the family returned to these shores around two centuries later (after exploits in Barbados,

In the shadow of the spire of Buckfastleigh Church stands 'The Sepulchre', final resting place of the Cabells of Brook Manor (q.v. 1655).

Antigua and the Leeward Islands) and one of his descendants is buried at Sampford Spiney.

1658 Hele's Charity is founded by Elize Hele. One of the properties owned by the charity is Collytown (or Collaton) Farm in Sheepstor.

1659 Thomas Menhere purchases the manor of Lydford.

1660 Following the restoration of the monarchy, the Forest of Dartmoor and the manor of Lydford once again revert to the Crown. It is granted in trust to Richard Arundel for Margaret Slanning, daughter of the Sir Nicholas who was its legal possessor (q.v. 1634) before the civil war. She is also granted all the profits from the stannary courts. ◆ John Grenville, Earl of Bath, becomes Lord Warden of the Stannaries. ◆ John Avent is steward of Plympton Manor at a view of Lee Moor bounds.

1661 Robert Toope assigns the "Tenemt in Shipstor called Hallintowne" (the tenement in Sheepstor called Hellingtown) to Thomas Farlew.

1662 William Watts and John Twigg are appointed bread weighers and ale tasters for the manor of Bickleigh.

1663 A new wing is added to the longhouse at Higher Dittisham, Walkhampton.

1664 Ponsworthy Bridge is in need of repair, so a brief is issued and collectors go round all the parishes in the south Devon district in order to raise monies for its rebuilding. The Buckland-in-the-Moor churchwardens contribute the princely sum of 5d! It is not until two years later that enough money has been raised, the bridge repaired and a datestone emplaced in the newly-built parapet.

1665 John Endacott, first Governor of Massachusetts, dies. Born in Chagford, John had sailed for New England from Weymouth in 1628.

1666 Sir Gervase Lucas devises a scheme for enclosing considerable tracts of land on Dartmoor for the use of the king. The commoners of Devon soon put him in his place! The proposals are speedily dropped. ◆ Abraham Peeke is sworn in as tithingman for the manor of Walkhampton.

1667 The Great Fire of London had occurred the previous year. Nothing to do with Dartmoor? Perhaps not directly, but by this year the following victims had somehow managed to make their way the 250+ miles to Mary Tavy Parish, where they received some alms from the churchwarden – "Paid to a woman great with child her home burnt in London 2s"; "Paid to women and children, their house burnt in London 3d".

1668 Richard and Prethesay Eles of Broadhempston sell 40 acres of land at Dryewells, Horsepark, Broadlands, Oak Parks and Groundhill, "sometime part of the Manor of Jordan Mallett", Widecombe, to Peter Ilbert of Hursdon. The selling price is £143 (q.v. 1744).

1669 The Bishop of Exeter bestows £20 to Drewsteignton "towards ye building of a dwelling house for ye poore of ye Parish". ◆ The Duke of Tuscany passes through Horrabridge, recording in his diary that it is a hamlet comprising "a few houses thatched with straw".

1670 Two rather unusual marriages take place in Holne – John Hannaford marries Susan Hannaford, his master's widow; and Edward Foster marries his servant maid, Welting Honnewell.

1671 A rather strange-looking map of Dartmoor tinworks is published in a volume of *Philosophical Transactions*.

1672 Richard Hill is the seneschalle (steward) of Dunstone Manor.

1673 Anthony Trennamen is the earliest known occupier of Yestor Green Farm.

1674 Robert Herrick dies and is buried at Dean Prior. His mural tablet can be seen (with difficulty!) in the church, there is a (now fallen) modern headstone to him in the graveyard and a window was also erected to his memory in relatively modern times.

1675 Richard Lambshead buys "a room called the Shopp with a dwelling house adjoining, the orchard adjoining, a little herbgarden, and the fields called Broomparke, Waterparke, Wood, Lower & Higher Gratney", at Higher Brembley, Ilsington.

1676 A religious census taken in the deanery of Plympton records that Buckland Monachorum is the only Dartmoor parish within the deanery which has any non-conformists – it has just 12, out of a total population of 435. The smallest parish is Sheepstor, with a population of only 68 (note that for the purposes of the census it is likely that only adults over 16 years of age were considered). ◆ Edward Meade becomes Nicholas Slanning's tenant at Ditsworthy Warren.

1677 Joseph Luscombe sells his share in "a certain tynworke mine called old beame otherwise outcombeme otherwise liteltors worke pit" to Edward Maunder.

1678 Sir Francis Drake of Buckland writes to Sir Nicholas Slanning of Bickleigh complaining that one of the latter's servants has been poaching Drake's salmon. ◆ James Poppen, from Cornwood, is impressed into service with the Navy.

1679 Josias Calmady becomes MP for Okehampton.

1680 James Yonge describes the church at Brentor thus – "Brent Tarr is a church on a very high hill I believe nearest heaven of any church in England" (this was true when he wrote these words, although Princetown Church is today a little nearer to heaven than Brentor).

1681 Non-conformist minister William Knapman is buried in Throwleigh C of E churchyard.

1682 Walter Langsford of Cockstorre, Peter Tavy, leases South Goldsworthy to Walter Colborn.

1683 Rev Thomas Bowen, vicar of Walkhampton, opens a new route to the church, Elbow Lane, and erects a granite stile at its southern end. Part of the datestone erected at the same time remains in the wall to this day.

1684 A cottage in Cornwood is razed to the ground by a fire. Unfortunately, it is the home of the parish clerk, and the pre-1685 registers, and other parish documents in his care, are destroyed in the blaze. ◆ A stone is built into the parapet of Drakeford Bridge recording that "This Bridg was Repard by the Covnty 1684".

1685 A royal warrant establishes the Devonshire Regiment's precedence as the 11th Foot. The 'Bloody Eleventh' was disbanded 273 years later (and amalgamated with the Dorset Regt to form the Devon & Dorset). ◆ Richard Dunning of Walkhampton writes a pamphlet entitled *A Plain & Easie Method shewing how the Office of Overseer of the Poor may be managed, whereby it may be £9,000 advantage to the County of Devon.* ◆ William Savery of Cornwood, and others, are arrested on suspicion of being "disaffected towards the government" (if this had still been enforcible three centuries later nearly the entire population of the country would have been imprisoned!).

1686 Walter Northmore pays a consideration of £31 to take on the lease of "Eastonden otherwise Collaton and the third part of one meadow called Redemede Lyeing in Shipstor...and...a certaine meadow called woeside meade ...in Meavy". The rent is just £1.

1687 William and Ann Creber are married in Walkhampton on the 29th of June. This might not strike readers as an especially remarkable event, save for the fact that, rather unusually, it is recorded on the headstone to the couple. To be seen in Walkhampton churchyard, this further states that they lived happily together for nearly 62 years. They died in 1749 and 1752 respectively.

1688 Sir Nicholas Slanning is appointed Vice Warden of the Stannaries.

1689 The previous year the inhabitants of Wapsworthy were presented in the Lydford court for the west quarter for permitting Wapsworthy Hedge or Fence "iuxta Forest de Dartmore" to be in a decayed state. The court rolls of this year record that the fence has been repaired. ◆ A deed records that "Witton Downe tynworke [was] claymed pitched and entered by Joanne Taprill widdow".

1690 Charles Palmer, carpenter, becomes Henry Walter's tenant at Downes House in Horndone tenement, Mary Tavy.

1691 William Warden is whipped at Whitchurch for being a "wandering rogue" and is ordered to be carried by the constables from parish to parish all the way back to Hertfordshire. He does not get far on his journey – he dies whilst being carried on horseback over Blackdown only a day or so later, and is buried at Mary Tavy – "at night", as the burial entry records.

1692 11s 3d is collected in the parish church of Bradford, Yorkshire, "upon Letters Patent [more commonly known as a Brief] to the inhabitants of Chagford in Devonshire". Melton-on-the-Hill, also in Yorkshire, collects 2s 10d. The occasion which necessitated the issuing of the brief was a fire in the Dartmoor town. ◆ The manor of Ivybridge is sold by William Drake to John Rogers for £3,500.

1693 John Doidge sells Monkiston in Brentor to Walter Nicholls for £100.

1694 John Rogers buys South Hele and Blachford.

1695 Celia Fiennes describes Ashburton as "a poor little town – bad was the best inn". She later passes through "a little place called Dean" where "the lanes are exceeding narrow".

1696 Nicholas Leaman and Henry French are the new owners of one of the tenements at Higher Cator, having purchased it the previous year from Thomas Hamlyn

1697 The manor of Buckland Monachorum, comprising 48 messuages, 3 tofts, 3 water mills, 1 fulling mill, 1 stamping mill, 52 gardens, 58 orchards, 126 acres of land, 39 acres of meadow, 95 acres of pasture, 37 acres of wood, and 1,132 acres of heath and furze, plus rights to hold courts in Horrabridge, Buckland Town, Roborough Down, Walkhampton, Sampford Spiney and Buckland Monachorum, is sold for £800.

1698 The parishioners of Buckland-in-the-Moor beat the bounds of the manor. A full list of all of those who attended the beating survives, together with a list of the names of the bond marks. ◆ John Hole of Drewsteignton is killed in a gunpowder explosion at the Blackaller limekilns.

1699 John Rogers of Blachford is elected MP for Plymouth and is created a baronet, the first of ten of his family to hold the title. ◆ The borough of Plymouth pays £2 "towards defraying the charges of putting upp Morrestones on Dartmoor in the way leading from Plymouth to Exon for guideing of Travellers passing that way". ◆ The delightfully-named little parcels of land called Spanging, Mary Island and Keep-a-Little are bequeathed to Mary Tavy Church by James Cole.

******

The Eighteenth Century

1700 The Rook Charity is founded by the Fortescues of Hanger, Cornwood, who bequeath the rent of Wakeham's Rook Farm to be spent on blankets and clothing for the poor at Christmas.

1701 Charles Bonville, Earl of Radnor, becomes Lord Warden of the Stannaries, but is replaced after only six months by John (later Baron) Granville.

1702 Lady Modyford founds a school at Buckland Monachorum.

1703 Defendants in a tithe suit brought by the rector of Lydford claim that it costs £20 to enclose a newtake in the Forest, but that such newly-enclosed land will not yield more than £1 p.a. return.

1704 Harford spends £9 8s 3d on repairing the roof of the church, around 75% of the total expenditure on church-related items this year. The massive total of 11,000 shindlestones (roof slates) are bought at a cost of £2 15s, and 4,000 lath nails for 5s 4d. Other sundry items bring the purchases up to £3 18s 1d, and the remainder of the total is taken up by labour costs at 1s 4d (7p) per day.

1705 Francis Godolphin becomes Lord Warden of the Stannaries.

1706 Samuel Bulteel lets Downes House in Horndon, Mary Tavy, to George Mudge, the village blacksmith. In the deed Bulteel describes himself as a "sugar refiner of Plymouth".

1707 There are two sides to the histories of most of the well-known Devon gentry families. The Drakes obviously need no introduction here, and during this period Francis Drake (great grandson of Thomas, brother of *the* Sir Francis) is lord of the manors of Buckland Abbey, Meavy and Nutwell, amongst other places. But I wonder how many readers have heard of Joan Drake?...She receives poor relief of a shilling (5p) a week from the Whitchurch overseers.

1708 Rev Joseph Rowe is buried at Buckland Monachorum. Quite remarkably, he had been the vicar there since 1646. ◆ Hugh Boscawen, Viscount Falmouth, becomes Lord Warden of the Stannaries. ◆ Richard Sleman becomes the tenant of Elizabeth Modyford (lady of the manor of Bickleigh) at Smallacombe, in Sheepstor, at a rent of 13s 4d p.a.

1709 A brief issued to raise monies for "Poor Palatines" raises the substantial sum of £3 5s 1d when read at South Molton. The parishioners of South Tawton are not so generous, and between them they donate just a shilling to the cause.

1710 Although not directly associated with Dartmoor as such, an inventory carried out in this year is of related interest. It lists the goods and chattels of the Kitley Estate left by the late Edmund Pollexfen, from a total of £1846 "cash in his possession" down to the minutiae such as two keives, one dropper and a tunner in the cellar, valued at £1 1s 6d. The inheritor of the estate is William Bastard of Gerston, who is also lord of the manor of Buckland-in-the-Moor.

1711 Ellen Mabbott of Shaugh Prior dies and leaves behind a mystery which has never been satisfactorily resolved. Her tombstone (now destroyed) recorded that she left £50 a year to the poor of the parish; the Charity Commissioners have no record of such a bequest ever having been made. ◆ The mortality rate at Widecombe suddenly doubles, to 49 burials, the reason for which is recorded thus by the clerk – "This yeare the small pock rain'd very much".

1712 A brief for a fire at Hastings read out in Meavy Church raises just 8d in donations. At South Tawton 2s 6d is collected on the same brief.

1713 The little Chapel of St Mary's is built at South Zeal, perhaps on the foundations of a much earlier guild chapel.

1714 Upon the accession of his father to the throne, George Augustus becomes the first Hanoverian Duke of Cornwall.

1715 Walter Crossman becomes the Maristow Estate's tenant at "A Cott on Lowery Moor", a reference to what was more usually known as East Lowery. The buildings of the smallholding, one of the earliest tenements at Lowery, established in the 13th century, are now in a totally ruinous condition.

1716 Richard Atwell becomes the Maristow Estate's tenant at the tiny tenement called Croftshead. His lease is the earliest documented reference to the tenement which has so far been found. The rent is just 2s (10p) p.a.

1717 Robert Pearse agrees to spend £10 in repairing the "water mill and tenement" at Lydia Mill as part of his payment for a lease on the property, which is signed the following year.

1718 Lady Modyford bequeaths in her will (written in 1718, though she did not actually die in this year) £200 to be equally divided between the parishes of Buckland Monachorum, Walkhampton, Bickleigh and Shaugh Prior, the interest to be spent on bread which was to be handed out every Sunday after morning service to the poor of the parishes who received no parochial relief.

1719 John Nosworthy of Widecombe is convicted for "the Swearing of

Eleven Oaths" (!) and is fined a shilling for each offence.

1720 Hedgehogs at Harford are in for a particularly bad time this year – 49 of them are killed by zealous parishioners as part of the policy of killing animals and birds perceived as 'vermin'. The outcome is that the churchwardens pay out 7s 6d (37½p) for hedgehogs, out of a total of 9s 6d expended by them on 'vermin control' this year.

1721 The church at Bovey Tracey sells one of its bells to Woodbury for £46 10s.

1722 The ace of diamonds is the next card to be turned over in a wager during a gambling party at Wonson Manor. The card costs John Northmore his entire estate, save for the manor house itself.

1723 Following the surrender of the lease of Thomas Collihall, deceased, the property at Trehill, Drewsteignton, is let by William Carew to William Easterbrook of Moreton on a three-life lease. The rent is just 7s 6d p.a., two capons on the Feast of St Michael and a heriot of the best beast or 10s (50p) payable upon the deaths of each of the lives. The terms of the lease include the usual covenants, amongst which are the more or less standard clauses bidding Easterbrook to perform suit of service to the courts held in the manor of Drewstainton or Tainton Drew.

1724 Upon the death of the last of the Modyfords, the vast Maristow Estate passes to Peter Heywood. ◆ Thomas Hele is arrested for beating and wounding Elizabeth Woodward at her alehouse in Cornwood.

1725 The 2nd "Act Against Profane Cursing & Swearing" is brought onto the statute books and, as one of its decrees, stipulates that it is to be read out in churches throughout the land on four days in the year; every church has to buy a copy. The Ugborough churchwardens pay 3d for theirs.

1726 John Dunning, son of John of Gnatham, Walkhampton, marries Agnes, daughter of Henry Jutsam. Three years later their son, another John, is born. It was the latter who was later to become Lord Ashburton. ◆ Hugh Smerdon conveys the tenements of Drywells and Uphill to his son, also Hugh, upon the latter's marriage to Duns (or Dewens) Hamlyn.

1727 William Nichols of Ditsworthy is registered as the occupier of what is intriguingly entitled "Little Yellowmead or the Blowing Mill Tenement". In the immediate preceding years this property was simply known as Little Yealamead, and the following year it reverts to its former title.

1728 Walter Radcliffe leases Hill Town in Peter Tavy to Elizabeth Taverner. ◆ John Browne of Moreton, serge weaver, sells Alexander Whiteway jnr, woolcomber, a messuage comprising

The ruins of the fortified manor house at Gidleigh, built by the Prouz family in 1324 (q.v. 1729).

three dwellings, a malthouse, a dry and a courtlage, plus appurtenances etc "at Batt & Barry near the Towns End at Moreton". The selling price is £160.

1729 At about this time most of Gidleigh Castle, built in 1324, and in reality a fortified manor house rather than a true castle, is demolished, its stones taken for the building of Gidleigh Barton nearby.

1730 Richard Geels pays £12 to Mary Dean for his new lease on Outhome Farm.

1731 A sentence against Dame Mary Rogers of Blachford, Cornwood, which had been imposed by the ecclesiastical court of Totnes in 1726, and confirmed by hearings held in the consistory court at Exeter in the same year and in the Court of Arches in 1729, is reversed upon a final appeal to the Court of Delegates, which awards Sir John Rogers the £300 costs of the suit and appeals. Two peers, three judges, two bishops and four doctors hear the case. And the subject of this protracted lawsuit, which had been ongoing for no less than eight years, and which had swallowed up hundreds of pounds in legal costs? – a row of hat pegs on the Blachford pew in Cornwood Parish Church, which had been sawn off by churchwarden W. Savery in 1723!!

1732 Jeffery Warring leases the Dunridge tenement from Waldo Calmady, the property described as being situated "in the north and south part of the way there leading from Harrowbridge to Sampford Spiney Church". The annual rent is 21s 4d. ◆ Jurors at the Buckland Monachorum manor court complain that the ducking stool and stocks are not being kept in repair.

1733 For a consideration of £50 Thomas Smaley becomes the tenant at Merivale Farm, on a 99-year lease at a rent of 10s (50p) p.a.

1734 Waltham Savery is convicted of "chiding and brawling" in the churchyard at Cornwood. ◆ Rather more seriously, a man called Skinner is indicted for the murder of John Taylor in Ashburton. ◆ Colonel John Schutz becomes Lord Warden of the Stannaries.

1735 Pascho Nute of Buckland Monachorum is drowned and a headstone erected to him in the local graveyard. Made by Solomon Oliver, it is the oldest surviving headstone in any Dartmoor graveyard which bears the name of the monumental mason who supplied it.

1736 J. Tabb of Cornwood leases the manor mills at Ivybridge from the Blachford Estate, one of the conditions of his lease being that he does not rent another grist, or flour, mill within a radius of 20 miles.

1737 Parishioners at Holne agree that their churchwardens should from henceforth pay 10s 6d for the killing of a fox.

Pascho Nute's footstone in Buckland Monachorum churchyard; the matching headstone, seen in the background, records the date of his death (q.v. 1735).

1738 The earliest known record of the dedication of the church at Belstone, said to be to St Mary the Virgin, appears in Ecton's *Thesaurus, the Valuation of Church Livings for the purpose of Queen Anne's Bounty.* ◆ George Fuge, blacksmith, becomes the new owner of Monkiston and Stagshead in Brentor.

1739 It is sometime around this year that the farm hitherto called Harris, in Sheepstor, first becomes known as Narrator, a name which the locality retains to this day. ◆ Meanwhile, the Crebers take over at nearby Outholme, where successive generations of the family are to farm for the next century.

1740 A huntsman of Slade, Cornwood, is attacked and devoured by his pack of hounds when he visits the kennels one night, the dogs not recognising him in the darkness.

1741 John Cummins, a 20-year old apprentice, has had enough of working under John Elford of Sheepstor, and runs away. Cummins is described in a report in the *Sherborne Mercury* as being of "reprobate life and conversation", so perhaps Elford was glad to be rid of him anyway!

1742 Thomas Pitt becomes Lord Warden of the Stannaries.

1743 An infant abandoned on the doorstep of Sortridge Manor is christened Mary Whitchurch, taking her surname from the parish in which she was found.

1744 Hugh Smerdon buys some closes of land called Drywells etc (q.v.

1668) from William Ilbert for £195, plus "one maydore of gold".

1745 Sir John Rogers of Blachford dies. He is buried at Cornwood, where also are to be seen the graves of his wife, Dame Mary, and other members of the family.

1746 Richard Seldon, woodturner, leases a house at the south-west corner of the Ivy Bridge, from the Rogers of Blachford, the first of four generations of the family to occupy the property. His grandson, John Seldon, converted the house to the Kings Arms c1825 (the pub is presently called The Exchange).

The Exchange, Ivybridge (q.v. 1746).

1747 These years mark the end of an era in Sheepstor. In order to settle a large mortgage debt Walter Elford conveys the whole of the manor and free hamlet of Sheepstor, and all his rights and privileges etc, to Robert Tapson and Thomas Jones and their heirs and assigns for ever. A few years later Narrator is sold to William Willcocks, and the residue of the manor and rights to hold the court leet, or view of frankpledge, etc to Richard Northmore. The following year (see below) Longstone's reign as an independent manor is also brought to a close.

1748 The death of John Elford of Sheepstor effectively brings to an end Longstone's status as an independent manor. He dies intestate and without issue, the inheritance going to Walter Yonge, grandson of the Walter Elford who lost the manor of Sheepstor in 1747 (see above). The reign of the Elfords as lords of Sheepstor had lasted 230 years, but that of the Northmores was to last only 72 years.

Reconstruction of Longstone Manor, based on a 19th century scale plan in the City of Plymouth & West Devon Record Office (q.v. 1747).

© J. E. Wood, 1871

1749 Mary Foot of Ashburton is presented at the manor court for violently driving away two of her husband's pigs and "causing two other people's pigs to run off to his disadvantage".

1750 The clams at Ouley and Glase (Owley and Glazebrook) are repaired by John Dunning of Ugborough at a cost of 5s 2d.

1751 James Waldegrave becomes Lord Warden of the Stannaries.

1752 John Dunning, later Lord Ashburton, becomes a student at Middle Temple.

1753 Walter Radcliffe mortgages the manor of Longford, Whitchurch, to William Edgecombe of Tavistock. As is customary for the period, the term is for 1,000 years – although it did not quite last that long! The principal sum and interest was cleared in 1788, by which time the original mortgagor had died (c1774) and the residue of the debt reassigned to John Carpenter. ◆ The tenants of Blachford Manor beat the bounds of Staldon Moor, probably as a result of a suit brought the previous year by a Sheepstor inhabitant against Sir John Rogers for illegally distraining his cattle and sheep depastured there.

1754 A "View and Perambulation of ye Borough and of ye Parish of Lydford" is undertaken.

1755 A new milestone is erected on the Tavistock-Lydford road, a mile from the former town, at a total cost of 13s 6d for the carriage of the stone from Dartmoor, for "facing and figureing ye milestone", and for erecting it. ◆ A wooden board is erected in the Ringer's Gallery at Buckland Monachorum Church, which proclaims that "We ring the Quick to Church, the Dead to Grave".

1756 The Plymouth-Exeter road is turnpiked.

1757 The East Birch Torr bounds, pitched by Jacob Rowe and John Roberts, are proclaimed and granted at the stannary court in Chagford. Three years earlier the same two men had pitched the Challacombe bounds, and three years before that George and Gustavus Gidley had pitched the Birch Tor tin bounds, both granted at the respective stannary courts. The three setts were, in the 1850s, to be incorporated with the other setts and bounds worked under the unified New Birch Tor & Vitifer Mining Company.

1758 Elizabeth Chubb and Joan Baker are just two of the spinners working for a pittance in the Ugborough workhouse. The workhouse manager is Philip Rogers who, aside from overseeing the work of the female inmates, is also responsible for sending the men to work on the roads.

1759 Richard Worth of Walkhampton buys a copy of a small religious book and seems determined to keep it, writing on the flyleaf – "Richard Worth His Book September 28th Day 1759. Richard Worth of Walkhampton Parish in the County of Devon His Book If this Book it Should be Lost and any one this Book do finde pray be so Loving and So kind To bring him back to Me again 1759.

Steal Not this Book for fear of Shame
for under Neath you'l See My Name
Richard Worth"

1760 John Colwell, churchwarden at Bridford, is killed whilst bellringing. Becoming entangled in the bell rope, he is at first carried upwards by the huge weight of the swinging bell, and then thrown headlong onto the stone floor of the tower by the downswing.

1761 John Giles, the tithingman, collects the 3s (15p) venville rent from Sheepstor Parish on behalf of the Duchy. The annual rate is the same as it had been for two and a half centuries (and probably for very much longer). ◆ An epidemic sweeps through South Tawton and 69 people are buried in the graveyard this year – 40 of them are children. The death rate reverts to its more usual level the following year, with just 27 burials taking place in 1762.

1762 A font of Portland stone is made for Chagford Church, at a cost of £3 3s. It has since been replaced by a granite one of 1857 vintage. ◆

The Tavistock Turnpike Trust is established. ◆ John Stephens of Peter Tavy commits suicide. He is buried near Broadmoor Corner, where his rough-hewn memorial stone may still be seen. ◆ Thomas Tyrwhitt is born in Essex.

1763 Humphrey Morice becomes Lord Warden of the Stannaries. ◆ The bells of Ugborough Church are recast by Billbie, bellfounder of Collumpton.

1764 John Tindall, curate of Brentor for the past 28 years, dies. ◆ The long-abandoned farmstead of Old Pyles is let to William Isaac, his lease including "common of pasture for of all manner of beasts and cattle" and rights to turbary on "All that Moor Waste or Common Ground called Harford Moor alias East Harford Moor" together with "All that one large Close of Land and Pasture...called higher Old Pyles".

1765 A Tavistock hotelier writes in a letter: "we had the greatest concourse of people I ever saw and at least fifty carriges...a great number sat up all night for want of beds as all the inns were full". And the great occasion which gives rise to these great multitudes descending on the area? – horse racing on Whitchurch Down, sponsored by the Duke of Bedford! ◆ The clapper bridge at Peek Mill is repaired, most of the work being done by John and Christopher Screech.

1766 A very curious alternative name for the plot of fields called Blackhay, or Jobbers, makes its first appearance in the Sheepstor rate lists, which describes the property as "Hallington also Hold Ischale". The name, in fact, turns out to be a rather odd alternative (mis)spelling for Holditch Hall.

1767 This year sees the beginnings of the long-running dispute between James Modyford Heywood of Maristow and Walter Radcliffe of Tamerton, Peter Tavy and Whitchurch etc over fishing rights on the River Tavy. The dispute was not finally settled until 1794!!

1768 Buckland Monachorum Parish spends 10s (50p) on "Setting up Bond Stones on Roborough Down". ◆ The population of Cornwood Parish is recorded as being 524 (this figure might represent adults aged 16 and above only).

1769 John Dunning, later Lord Ashburton, buys Spitchwick and Natsworthy Manors.

1770 During the summer months the men in the Ugborough workhouse are engaged in repairing the roads and tracks around Glaze Water, Cutwill and Cheston, working a six-day-week, ten or eleven hours a day.

1771 William Windeat senior, who was to spend at least 25 years of his life in the Ugborough workhouse, is joined by two new inmates just five days before Christmas – his son and grandaughter, William and Elizabeth.

1772 John Vickry is elected Mayor of Okehampton for the sixth time.

1773 Edmund Moon is contracted to build "two Bridges in the Forrest of Dartmoor at a place called two Bridges" for £65. Completed in 1774, they had to be entirely rebuilt the following year, and these replacements were themselves destroyed in a flood just nine years later, in 1784.

1774 Walter Elford exhibits his painting entitled *View of the River Tavy in Devon* at the Royal Academy.

1775 Josiah Wedgewood visits North Wheal Robert, Sampford Spiney, to inspect its cobalt ores, but no purchases by his Staffordshire pottery follow.

1776 A survey and valuation of (part of?) the manor of Drewsteignton records the following tenants in occupation at the various properties: William Easterbrook, Trehills; R. Powell, West Wood Farm; John Hill, New Fillett Tenement; Robert Luxton, North East Hills; James Battishill, Veet Messuage and Farm; Mary Brock, East Wood Tenement; Thomas Collihill, North West Hills and Overland. The total extent is just 272½ acres, the gross yearly value £107 7s.

1777 N. T. Carrington, author of *Dartmoor* and other poems, is born in Plymouth.

1778 Edward Hamlyn of Scobbotor dies possessed of 4 cows, 2 calves, an ox, 2 heifers, 5 bullocks, 4 horses, 20 couples of ewes and lambs, 24 sheep, 2 pigs and a goose. ◆ In the same year James Coombe of Ashburton meets an untimely end, drowning after having fallen into a tan pit.

1779 A violent storm at Manaton tears part of the north wall of the church tower away, sends masonry and broken timber crashing through the roof of the nave and blows in the east window, badly damaging the altar.

1780 The last indigenous stag on Dartmoor is killed after a 5½ hour chase beginning at Brook Wood, Buckfastleigh.

1781 449 seams of stones are used to repair Yalland Brook Lane in Ugborough.

1782 Joseph Northmore is presented before the Buckland Monachorum manor court for overstocking Roborough Down.

1783 George Legge, Viscount Lewisham, becomes Lord Warden of the Stannaries. He is later to become the Earl of Dartmouth.

1784 William Bennet, the composer and organist, starts teaching the choir singers at Buckland Monachorum, in a 26-day stint for which he is paid 6s (30p) a day, plus two guineas (£2 2s) for his keep and that of his horse. He also teaches the singers at Ugborough and other Dartmoor churches during this period.

1785 The recipe for Ashburton pop, which sold for 2d per bottle, is lost upon the death of the last brewer of the beer.

1786 The original boards commemorating the Great Storm of Widecombe of 1638 are replaced by new ones and hung in the chancel (they now hang in the tower). Peter and Silvester Mann are the churchwardens.

1787 Judge Francis Buller buys Prince Hall from Christopher Gullet, and sets about squandering his money on attempts to turn the waste into fields of waving wheat and barley.

1788 The Bishop of Exeter grants a petition to representatives of the inhabitants of Ivybridge to build a chapel there, on account of the great distance of the village from the nearest churches at Harford, Cornwood, Ugborough and Ermington (between which parishes Ivybridge was at that time divided), "by reason whereof the Lord's Day was most shamefully neglected and profaned" by the inhabitants. The new chapel was licensed for Divine Service the following year. ◆ Meanwhile, in one of these parishes, Ugborough, the tithes are recorded as being £101 0s 9d: by the time of the Tithe Commutation of 1844 they had risen to £185, reflecting the increase in the value of land in the district.

1789 Rev John Swete goes on a tour of northern Dartmoor. Amongst the places he visits is the Drewsteignton cromlech, where he describes several stone rows and a circle in fields to the west. All trace of their existence had gone by the time Ormerod surveyed the area in the 1870s. ◆ Abraham Giles of Lethertor becomes tithingman for Walkhampton Manor. ◆ William H[e]ard, apprentice to John Kellond, is killed by a horse, which latter is forfeited (as a deodand) to James M. Heywood, lord of the Maristow Manors.

1790 Two "diricting posts" are erected at a cost of 6s by the waywardens of Buckland-in-the-Moor. One of these guidestones survives, standing on the verge of the junction at Stone Cross, the only known dated guidestone on the whole of Dartmoor. ◆ Ann Eliza Kempe is born on Christmas Day. Not an especially notable event, perhaps, save for family and friends of course. She is, however, familiar to many readers, but under a different name – for the infant is the future Mrs Bray of *Tamar & Tavy* fame. She died in 1883.

1791 The Ponsfords become lords of the manor of Drewsteignton.

1792 Susanna Willis becomes a servant of James Wotton, a butcher of Ugborough. Her starting wages are just £3 a year, increased to £3 10s in 1793.

The prehistoric cromlech at Drewsteignton known as Spinster's Rock (q.v. 1789).

1793 A new "cross tree", a yew, is planted at Widecombe. (This died in 1860 and a new one was planted in its place.) ◆ 21 cock fights (described in contemporary adverts as "battles") take place in the London Inn at Ivybridge (then in Harford Parish) on March 13 and 14. The landlord/owner is one Henry Rivers who, in his more regular advertising, proclaims that he has "neat post chaises" available for hire by the gentry. ◆ Polwhele writes of Sticklepath that it is a "mean place, the cottages falling to decay and thatched in a slovenly manner".

1794 Horse races are held again on Henlake Down, as they had been for many years. The squires of Slade and Blachford win silver cups in two races. The foundations of the stand may still be seen on the down to this day.

1795 John Laskey writes an account of a four-day journey across Dartmoor and is evidently singularly unimpressed with much of what he sees, describing the moors above Cornwood, for example, as the "fag-end of Nature's work"! ◆ At about the same time James Younge visits Lydford (also on Laskey's itinerary) and describes its inhabitants as "rude and ill bred". The people of neighbouring Brentor are similarly "very rude and brutish"! ◆ The Ugborough parish constable is paid £1 11s 11½d "Towards taking a Highwayman".

1796 The end of an era in Walkhampton – after a period of occupation spanning at least five centuries there are soon to be no more Atwills at Welltown. Early in the following year the last of the main line, Roger Atwill, bequeaths the freehold of this property to his nephew, Abraham Giles, who also receives Creaber in Tavistock. Deancombe is bequeathed to nephew Elias Giles.

1797 Dr W. Samford of Moreton is called upon to assist in the delivery of Martha Woodley's child. His fee for this service is a guinea, "plus two shillings and sixpence for the journey". ◆ John Pinsent leases the Kelly Mine sett from George Wills for "the mining of black lead or some other substance".

1798 Sir John Morshead becomes Lord Warden of the Stannaries. ◆ Ugborough inhabitants celebrate a great naval victory as the following entry in their churchwardens' accounts reveals – "For 31 Qurts ale and a pint when admiral Nelson beat the french fleet". The innkeeper's bill for supplying all of this liquor is a mere 10s 6d (52½p)!

1799 Richard Treleaven begins his diary, which he calls *Chronological Occurences in Moretonhampstead*. Later members of the family are buried in the Cross Street chapel, although there is no memorial to Richard in its tiny graveyard.

*****

The Nineteenth Century

1800 A survey of the manor of Buckland-in-the-Moor is undertaken, plotting all of the field names and acreages of the manor farms on a large map of the estate. As an archive source, the map is more valuable, and contains far more information, than the 1840 tithe map of the parish. ◆ Rear Admiral Sir John Willett Payne becomes Lord Warden of the Stannaries. ◆ Edward Shapter of Cornwood is the Chief Constable of the Ermington hundred.

1801 Jonas Coaker, later to become affectionately known as the Dartmoor Poet, is born at Hartiland. ◆ John Guest of Ugborough receives his income tax demand – the sum assessed for the previous year is just £2 5s (Guest was, by the way, one of the wealthier yeomen of the parish at the time!).

1802 John Perryman buys the freehold of Yeo Farm, Chagford, for £675 from Mrs Elizabeth Chave of Alphington.

1803 James Brooke, the First Rajah of Sarawak, is born in Bengal. ◆ Thomas Tyrwhitt becomes Lord Warden of the Stannaries. ◆ 55 stones are erected to mark the boundary between Ugborough and Harford, in dispute since 1782.

1804 The Buckland Monachorum overseers pay £9 19s 6d to a Dr Guineas "for Innockalating of 38 Person for the Smallpox".

1805 An inventory of goods owned by the church at Buckland Monachorum includes the following items for the church band – a bassoon, a violincello, two violins, two German flutes and two singing books.

1806 George Bidder, who was later to become famous as the 'Calculating Boy', is born in Moretonhampstead, the son of a mason. ◆ Polwhele publishes his *History of Devonshire.*

1807 The first French POW to be paroled to Moretonhampstead arrives in the town. ◆ William Courtenay of Walreddon writes to Rev Walter Radcliffe requesting that he act as trustee in his marriage settlement. The reverend graciously agrees, although it seems that it was not until some two years later that Courtenay felt moved to invite him to dine at Walreddon!

1808 Sir Massey Lopes buys Meavy Manor from the Drakes. ◆ The proprietors of the Virtuous Lady Mine are accused of leaving their leat on Roborough Down in a dangerous condition. The following year they pay a £2 fine to the Buckland Monachorum manor steward in mitigation for the offence.

1809 The Depot at Dartmoor (later Dartmoor Prison) is completed, at a cost of £74,000. Built to house POWs, who had previously been imprisoned on rotting hulks on the Hamoaze and elsewhere, its doors are first opened to 5,000 of these men who are force-marched up from Plymouth.

1810 George Giles takes over the post of land agent, conveyancer and steward for all the manors on the Maristow Estate, a position which he held until his death in 1859, aged 71. Buried at Bickleigh, his large chest tomb in the churchyard there bears an appropriate tribute to his service. ◆ Louis Ambrose Quantin, a lieutenant of the 44th Regt du Corps Imperial d'Artillerie de Marine, dies whilst a POW on parole to Moretonhampstead. Most of the important inhabitants of the town attend his funeral, together with 104 paroled French and Danish officers, and he is buried with full masonic honours.

1811 French POWs begin building the church at Princetown. ◆ Adverts in the *Sherborne Mercury* offer summer pasturing at Fox Torr, for 8s a bullock, 7s per yearling, 10s for mares and colts, and 10s per score of sheep, which latter would be depastured at Whiteworks. Remarkably, the ads proclaim that the land around Fox Torr is "free from all dangerous bogs"!!

1812 Rev Edward Atkins Bray becomes vicar of Tavistock, in which post he serves for the next 45 years. ◆ Thomas Tyrwhitt is knighted. (He died 21 years later, aged 71.) ◆ Francis Charles Seymour, Earl of Yarmouth and later Marquis of Hertford, replaces him as Lord Warden of the Stannaries. ◆ Oliver Palmer of Buckland Monachorum is murdered with a potato axe. ◆ 412 officers and men of the 11th Devonshire Regt, men from the southern Dartmoor parishes amongst them, go into battle at Salamanca. There are only 71 survivors. The regiment is from henceforth known as 'The Bloody Eleventh'.

1813 John Pooke and Peter Chaffe become landlords at the Saracen's Head (since enlarged, and now called the Two Bridges Hotel).

1814 Several American POWs are killed during a riot at Princetown jail. ◆ A survey and valuation of the New Fillett Estate in Drewsteignton, conducted on behalf of the Praeds, who had become the owners after the Carews had ceased to have an interest in the properties there, values the property at £17 yearly. Other Drewsteignton properties were surveyed at around this time, as it seems that the family wished to relinquish its relatively recently acquired holdings in this region – perhaps forseeing the onset of the major depression which was to follow in the post-Napoleonic era?

1815 James Holman Mason becomes rector of Widecombe, a post he was to hold for 45 years. ◆ The expenses incurred by the Sheepstor overseers this year, in one of the tiniest parishes on Dartmoor, are a shocking £56 17s 11d. In one or two exceptional years during this era they rocket to over £75.

1816 John Taylor is appointed secretary to the Wheal Friendship Mine committee. ◆ 5,000 people attend the Yealmpton funeral of John Bastard, lord of the manor of Buckland-in-the-Moor.

1817 Both of the Hilltowns at Peter Tavy are leased by Thomas Roskilly from Rev Walter Radcliffe.

1818 A son, christened Massey, is born to a well-known western Dartmoor family. He will become Sir Massey Lopes of Maristow, Bart, lord of the manors of Sheepstor, Walkhampton, Meavy, Shaugh Prior, Buckland Monachorum, Maristow, Tamerton Foliot and Bickleigh – one of the most powerful landowners in the district in late-Victorian times. ◆ Three villains, Pollard, Metters and Williams, rob the church at Buckland Monachorum.

1819 The author, Charles Kingsley, is born in the vicarage at Holne. ◆ The adventurers at Wheal Lopes and Wheal Vergeon mines are presented at the Bickleigh manor court for "not making a proper bridge over the new leat on Roborough Down". ◆ Meanwhile, "the Miners Leat in Parsons Lane" is the subject of complaints in the Meavy manor court, for being "not passable as it ought to be".

1820 Work commences on the construction of The Plymouth & Dartmoor Railway which, when opened two years later, ran from Crabtree, Plymouth to the granite quarries situated near Princetown. ◆ Haley Horton, one of many members of his family to bear the same Christian name, is buried at Cornwood, aged 74. The story of his life is similar to those of many tens of thousands of Dartmoor men and women who seldom, if ever, had occasion to venture far beyond the boundary of their home parish – his epitaph records that he was "Late of Lower Donaton in this Parish Where he was Born and Remaind and Died Decr 14 1820".

1821 Walter Northmore holds his final court leet, or view of frankpledge, as lord of the manor of Sheepstor. The following year he sells the manor to Henry Mervyn Baylay for just £200.

1822 Richard Fuke, William Bickle, Joseph Edmund, Richard Light, John Kivell, Henry Coram, Richard Piten and Alexander Sergent are paid 1s (5p) per day for working on the roads in Walkhampton Parish during the summer. A Mr Adams and a Mr Leaman are paid 6s a day on the occasions when their services are required with two horses and a cart for hauling roadstone etc. ◆ The new Yelverton-Tavistock turnpike road is opened. Details of the opening ceremony, attended by the Duke of Bedford and other dignitaries, are recorded in a letter written by John Bayly.

1823 Samuel Hannaford, returning from market with a nag which he had been coaxed into trading for his finer animal, hangs himself beside the road near Cumston (one account of the incident suggests that he might even have been saved by the timely intervention of a passer-by whom, however, apparently let Hannaford hang there for fear of being implicated in a crime). The spot is today still known as Hangman's Pit.

1824 George Bowden is engaged by the Ilsington waywardens to build a new bridge at Bagtor. His bill for the work, totalling just £13 10s, is entered in the annual highways' accounts the following Easter.

1825 Rev William Davy, curate of Lustleigh since 1786, gives a field near Moretonhampstead to the village to endow the first school in Lustleigh. A small building for the school is erected in the grounds of the churchyard under a faculty granted by the bishop of the diocese. ◆ Wheal Friendship pays out a total of £23,680 in dividends to its shareholders. ◆ A stone coffin and some human bones are unearthed from the floor of the nave of St Peter's, Buckland-in-the-Moor, conjectured, somewhat tenuously, to be the remains of William de Bokland who died in 1232.

1826 Sir M. M. Lopes grants a lease to Joseph Key and John Wilton to "dig search stream and try for Tin" on a parcel of land called Longstone Pitts in Sheepstor Parish. The rent is "one fifteenth part dish dole or share of all such tin as shall be there found". ◆ Meanwhile, some of Lopes' Walkhampton tenants are complaining about The Plymouth & Dartmoor Railway line blocking the track leading from Croftshead to Church Way.

1827 William Shillibeer, who had been schoolmaster at Walkhampton for 48 years, dies. His large chest tomb may be seen in the graveyard there. ◆ Teignhead Clapper Bridge is built, on the site of an older one destroyed by floods during the previous year.

1828 The annual Duchy courts are transferred from Lydford to Princetown. ◆ A number of poor persons are charged at the Meavy manor court for illegally making stacks of turf (peat turves) on Meavy Green, for which the overseer pays the court a shilling as acknowledgement for the offences.

1829 Hele Cross is rescued from its watery grave in the Bovey Brook by Rev Jones, curate of North Bovey.

1830 Mary Hannah, singlewoman of Ugborough, declares on oath in a settlement examination that she was "born on board a ship as she hath heard and believes...father was a soldier who was settled in South Brent...when she was seven years old she was bound out an

Teignhead Clapper Bridge emerges from the early morning mists (q.v. 1827).

Apprentice to Andrew Knight of South Brent, farmer...".

1831 The first threshing machine in Chagford is brought into use at Yeo Farm. However, the first wheeled conveyance is not used at the farm until a couple of years later!

1832 After much debate in Parliament, the manor of Cudlipptown is severed from Tavistock Parish and incorporated into that of Peter Tavy. ◆ Richard Willis of Ugborough, serving with the 43rd Regiment of Foot, is court-martialled and dishonourably discharged for "disgraceful and infamous conduct". ◆ New apparatus for weighing bread and measuring ale is delivered to the courts held in the manors of Bickleigh, Buckland Monachorum and Meavy.

1833 Sir William Courtenay, lord of the manor of Walreddon, leads the inhabitants of Whitchurch on a beating of their bounds. ◆ At the manor court in neighbouring Walkhampton, Walter King and Peter Reed are sworn in as bread weighers and ale tasters for the following year. ◆ Sir Ralph Lopes threatens legal action against John H. Gill for illegally digging for sand and gravel on Roborough Down.

1834 An 80-inch steam engine, built by Perram Foundry Co, is installed at Wheal Friendship to help dewater the deepest levels of the mine.

1835 The weekly *Mining Journal* is first published. ◆ Bound beaters of Bagtor Manor decide that a newly-erected stone in the col between Saddle Tor and Hey Tor is to be christened 'Irish', after William Irish of Bagtor. ◆ Ivybridge becomes a separate parish in its own right, taking in portions of Ugborough, Harford, Cornwood and Ermington.

1836 The Duchy issue a grant to Prenton, Trout and White to search for minerals within the Wheal Virgin sett. They had, perhaps, applied for the grant in response to an advert in the *Mining Journal* during the latter part of the previous year, which advertised a meeting to be held at the Duchy Hotel "for the purpose of receiving applications from parties desirous of obtaining setts to search for tin and other metals within the lands belonging to the Duchy of Cornwall".

1837 A Mr Helyer of Meavy wins the first prize of £2 in a series of Devon wrestling bouts at the Moretonhampstead Games. ◆ George Frean's application to open what he called a 'Gunpowder Manufactory' near Bickleigh is refused by Sir Ralph Lopes, lord of the manor, who would not countenance the introduction of "any thing of the kind into the peaceful Vale of Bickleigh". Seven years later, however, Frean's search for a site at last proved successful, when the powder mills were built on Duchy land near Postbridge.

The cottages at Powder Mills, built in 1844 (q.v. 1837).

1838 The new rectory at Belstone is completed, at a cost of £381.

1839 The Bible Christians Chapel at what was later named Providence Place is built at a cost of £136 7s 4d.

1840 The Moretonhampstead tithe apportionments record that the Dean & Chapter of Canterbury still hold the Doccombe Estate (q.v. 1170).

1841 Quicksilver, the Plymouth to London mail coach, becomes snowbound on the turnpike road near Ivybridge. ◆ Had the mail coach progressed a little further along the highway the driver could have stopped at the Buller's Arms in Dean Prior, where the appropriately named Nancy Beer is the landlady. ◆ The year '1841' is carved on a large boulder in the bed of the River Mewy just upstream from Norsworthy Bridge, but its significance remains a mystery.

1842 Prince Albert becomes Lord Warden of the Stannaries.

1843 The price of tin, which had been £150 per ton in 1814, is now just £60 a ton. Eylesbarrow Mine closes. James Henry Deacon is one of the major shareholders who loses money in the venture. ◆ The Iron Mine Company is fined at the Meavy manor court for leaving open a number of dangerous pits on Yennadon Common.

1844 A massive new waterwheel, 50ft diameter and 11ft breast, is brought into operation at Wheal Friendship, the largest wheel ever to be used at the site.

1845 Fire in Moretonhampstead destroys most of the commercial premises and houses in Cross Street and Fore Street; 50 families become homeless. ◆ The Warren House Inn is rebuilt on the opposite side of the road to the former New House Inn. ◆ The tithe commissioners are called in to arbitrate in a dispute between Whitchurch and Sampford Spiney over the parish boundaries on and around Pew Tor Common etc. ◆ The construction of the South Devon Railway, and the undesirable elements amongst the workforce engaged in this work, necessitates the appointment of extra constables at Ivybridge in order to protect the inhabitants and their property.

1846 Siward's Cross is thrown down and broken in half by two youths.

1847 The owners of Wheal Masseh and Walkhampton Consols mines on Fillice Down are again presented at the manor courts for "leaving dangerous pits open". Despite the fact that complaints had been continuing since as early as 1843, it seems that it was not until 1853 that George Giles, manor steward, wrote to the companies about this issue, after sheep had been killed falling into the pits and shafts. ◆ William Crossing is born.

1848 Samuel Rowe's *Perambulation of the Forest of Dartmoor* is published. ◆ The "mortal life" of Hariett Endacott, aged 15, is "terminated by means of a thunder storm", as her headstone in Belstone graveyard records.

1849 Charles Kingsley stays at the Three Crowns, Chagford and waxes lyrical about the "beautiful old mullioned and gabled inn [with] granite and syenite everywhere...looking out on the old churchyard...beyond [is] a wilderness of lovely hills and woods". During his visit to the area he writes the poem *Dartside* which, rather oddly considering its title, is penned whilst he is fishing on the North Teign.

1850 Levels at Wheal Friendship are opened up 1/2 mile underground, the deepest workings of any Dartmoor mine. ◆ Ashburton's ancient market house and bullring is demolished.

1851 The nationwide census records Sheepstor's largest ever population – just 126 souls live in the little parish! One and a half centuries later the figure was less than half this number. Ashburton's population, on the other hand, is recorded as 3,432, roughly the same as it is today. ◆ Dr Coker scathingly describes the steps cut on Hey Tor as permitting the "enervated and pinguedinous scions of humanity to gain the summit"!

1852 James Toop is paid 1s by the Whitchurch churchwardens for cutting a date stone for the stables during the previous year. The stone may still be seen, in the gable end of the building nearly opposite the main gate of the churchyard.

1853 Sir Edward Smirke becomes Vice Warden of the Stannaries. ◆ A 25lb package sent from Ivybridge to Paddington costs 9d. ◆ In this and the following year, the Duke of Somerset erects a new series of boundstones delineating his land in Ilsington and Widecombe. Those on Haytor Down, erected in this year, bear the names 'Old Jack', 'Victoria', 'Prince of Wales' and 'Duke Stone' (this latter stone, which had been lost, was replaced in 1995 as a memorial to the late Harry Starkey).

1854 Sir Ralph Lopes of Maristow dies; the estate passes to his son Massey. ◆ Dicker of Chagford supply the waterwheel for Yeo Mill.

1855 Bronze Age spearheads, now in the Exeter Museum, are found near Bloody Pool, which according to local lore was the site of a battle in ancient times. ◆ The Depot at Dartmoor (q.v. 1809) opens as a convict prison for the first time. ◆ George Worth and William Mashford contract with Walkhampton Parish to build a bridge at Riddipit Steps for £26 10s, today known as Lethertor Bridge.

1856 The foundation stone is laid for a new church at North Brentor.

1857 Christ Church, North Brentor, is consecrated by Bishop Phillpotts. ◆ The Parkers take over as lords of the manor of Cornwood (the present Delamore Estate).

1858 Prices of some commodities which may be purchased at Beck & Son, "Family Grocers, Tea, Coffee & Spice Dealers, Chemists Etc", of Ashburton – 1 qrt vinegar 2s, 1lb raisins 6d, loaf of bread 6d, 1lb sugar 7d, 1 orange 1d, 1lb coffee 1s 4d, a sponge cake 6d, a dozen eggs 1s 2d [12d = 1s = 5p].

1859 Sir James Brooke, Rajah of Sarawak, buys the Burrator Estate. He died there in 1868 and is buried in Sheepstor churchyard. Evidently the colour of the local stone was not to his liking – his

As befits a stone named after the reigning monarch, the 'Victoria' boundstone on Haytor Down is larger and more elegant than the others (q.v. 1853).

sarcophagus is carved from a single slab of Red Aberdeen granite. ◆ William Cotton visits Harford Church and describes its interior as having "green mould struggling everywhere against the sickly whitewash...granite pillars half cased up with deal like broken limbs in splints..." etc.

1860 The stone rows at Trowlesworthy are saved from destruction by the timely intervention of Rev W. J. Coppard, vicar of Plympton. ◆ Sheepstor Church is 'restored' (at least, that is what the Victorians called it!) and the tracery from the window of the south aisle is removed. Fifty-one years later, Rev Hugh Breton rescued the stones and used them for a canopy which was erected over St Leonard's Well.

1861 Charles Galland, butcher of Ashburton, sells most of his meats – beef, pork, veal, bullock tongue – at just 7½d (approx 3p) per lb; a sheep's trotter costs 1d, a calf's foot 2d, shin beef 4d per lb.

1862 The original market house in the square at Chagford is demolished. ◆ Henry Pelham, Duke of Newcastle, becomes Lord Warden of the Stannaries.

1863 Richard Williams, licensee of the Carpenter's Arms in Tavistock, is fined £1 for "harbouring prostitutes". At the same court, John Kerslake, innkeeper, is fined £5 for permitting "persons of notoriously bad character" to frequent his alehouse.

1864 How, or when, Jump came to be so called seems to be nowhere recorded, but this is the year in which it seems to have been officially changed to its current, more familiar name, as recorded in a Buckland Monachorum burial register entry noting the death of a Roborough inhabitant, "till this year called Jump".

1865 Edward Berkeley, Baron Portman, becomes Lord Warden of the Stannaries. ◆ Fourteen ponies escape during the autumn drift at Buckland-in-the-Moor.

1866 The Moretonhampstead & South Devon Railway opens its new station at Lustleigh. ◆ W. H. Thornton becomes rector of North Bovey, where he finds that many of the parishioners are violently disposed towards each other, although "the men have recently given up fighting on saturday nights"! Despite this somewhat ignominious start to his incumbency, he grew to like the place and stayed as rector there for 50 years. The parishioners obviously liked him, too, for in 1910 they gave a new pulpit to the church to commemorate his 80th birthday. ◆ Two miners driving on the 40 fathom level at Furze Hill Wood Mine inadvertently break through into part of the older workings, and water pours in through the breach. Six men and a young boy are killed.

1867 Rev W. Y. Daykin leases from the Duchy a parcel of land around

Nuns Cross and Plym Head to establish the Crane Hill Warren.

1868 Louisa C. Bradshaw buys the substantial part of Elford Town Farm for £1,475 from the liquidators of John Williams.

1869 Robert Dymond buys the manor of Dunstone (with Blackslade) from the Norrishes. The latter had only reigned as lords of the manor for a brief period, having purchased it from the Hamlyns in 1784.

1870 Misguided 'restorers' vandalise the interior of South Brent Church – what is said to have been the finest surviving medieval rood screen in Devon is torn from its mountings and consigned to a bonfire.

1871 Sir John Rogers, 8th Baronet, is created Lord Blachford of Wisdome. ◆ The rural dean is singularly unimpressed by Belstone Church, saying that "...the entrance porch is very dirty, poultry having been allowed to get in...unless the church is restored, it must fall...". ◆ J. E. Wood writes of the remains of a sundial over the porch at Sheepstor Church. It is, in fact, part of an ancient tomb for members of the Elford family.

The supposed sundial at Sheepstor (q.v. 1871).

© J. E. Wood, 1871

1872 James Ferguson resolves a question which had been puzzling antiquaries for many years, when he describes the Merrivale stone rows as portraying an army, or two armies, drawn up in battle array. Why this starkly obvious fact had hitherto been overlooked is rather a mystery for, as Ferguson observes, when considered in this light "the whole seems clear and intelligible". Strangely, some sceptics seem to dispute his findings!! ◆ A visitor to Sheepstor describes the village as being "a century behind in civilisation".

1873 The Prince of Wales inspects 10,000 troops on Roborough Down.

1874 Haytor Iron Mine raises 1,669 tons of ore valued at £1,500. ◆ The newly-formed Whitchurch School Board resolve to accept the tender from Messrs Dwelley & Son of Plymouth to prepare plans and specifications for building a new school at Whitchurch. The

The soldiers of Merrivale, drawn up in 'battle array' (q.v. 1872).

school is completed two years later and the board set a scale of weekly charges, ranging from 1d/2d for the child of a labourer under/over 5 years old up to 6d for the child of a farmer over 5 years old: lower rates apply for the third child or more from the same family and higher rates after children have passed certain standards. School-leaving age is set at 11, when most children went out to work or were apprenticed (but some, especially from the poorer families, worked before this age, illegally skipping school to earn a meagre wage).

1875 Wheal Friendship goes into liquidation, having operated at considerable annual losses for well over a decade. Remarkably, and perhaps uniquely amongst the downfall of former industrial giants of the era, it leaves no unsettled debts. The workers, of course, are the ones who have most to lose from its closure.

1876 The green at Sheepstor is let to William Andrews for 27s a year (later reduced to £1) on condition that it is stocked with bullocks only.

1877 Kelly College opens in Tavistock. ◆ A new waterwheel and stamps are installed at Steeperton Mine, purchased by Charles Langley at an auction of machinery at Hexworthy Mine.

1878 The standard price for a slate headstone is between £2 10s and £3 10s; a heading costs 1s 8d, bordering 1s 8d, gilding 1s 6d and words 2d each; an elaborately designed and inscribed 'SACRED' in the superscript costs 1s 8d, whilst an even more elegantly scrolled 'IN' costs 2s (10p). ◆ The rural dean writes in his visitation book of the "propriety of restoring the canopy to the font" at Shaugh Prior. The huge medieval carved oak canopy is rescued, having lain rotting in a nearby barn for some years, and restored to its rightful place shortly afterwards. The medieval rood screen was not so fortunate – it had been consigned to a bonfire a few years earlier.

1879 William Legassick of Sheepstor becomes the representative for that parish on the Roborough Highways Board.

1880 James Johnston MacAndrew of Lukesland is the driving force behind the restoration of Harford Church, not only helping to raise funds, but financing much of the rebuilding costs himself. The following year he finances the erection of the first purpose-built school in the village. ◆ Rev G. H. H. Hutchinson pays £80 p.a. to the Maristow Estate for the shooting rights throughout Meavy, Sheepstor and Walkhampton. In contrast, at the opposite end of the scale of rentals, William Shillibeer of Sheepstor pays a shilling a year "for leave to cross the river by clam". ◆ On the subject of clams, that at Mary Tavy is destroyed in a flood, as, too, is Hill Bridge, higher up the Tavy.

1881 Snowstorms in January and February block the Plymouth Leat, cutting off the water supply to the city for several weeks. The same thing was to happen exactly ten years later.

1882 E. Fearnley Tanner writes to the *Western Antiquary* on the subject of encroachment, which includes a proposal to "form an association called the Dartmoor Preservation Association, with the object of narrowly watching the Moor, protesting about anything we may think an invasion, and, if need be, taking action".

1883 Dewerstone Iron Mine, opened only three years previously, is put up for auction upon the collapse of the Ferro Ceramic Co Ltd which started the venture. Remains of the workings can be seen near Shaugh Bridge. ◆ The Princetown railway line is opened, much of it constructed upon the now-defunct trackbed of The Plymouth & Dartmoor Railway's section of line from Yelverton.

1884 Shortly after the closure of the graveyard to future burials, a "Table of Fees for the New Parish Cemetery at Buckland Monachorum" is issued. The cost of a common grave 6ft deep is 1s (5p), a headstone without inscription 5s, vaults 2s 6d per sq ft, inscription 1s 6d and the minister's fee 8s 6d.

1885 After another unusually mild winter on north Dartmoor the Sourton Ice Works is on the brink of collapse. It closes early the following year.

1886 Fire destroys part of Wistmans Wood, but the cause of the blaze is unknown.

1887 The Royal Oak Inn, Meavy, is said to be "badly supplied with drinks, often being without Ale for 2 or 3 days together and all owing to the management of the House". ◆ In the Queen's Jubilee year, many parishes on Dartmoor have a bonfire to celebrate the event. The inhabitants of Whitchurch get a little over-enthusiastic about this idea – their bonfire is 50 ft high, includes seven tons of ships' timbers and is saturated with 200 gallons of tar. It burns continuously for four days and three nights!

1888 Henry John Reynolds becomes Lord Warden of the Stannaries.

1889 St Michael of the Rock, Brentor, is repaired at a cost of £728. Forty skeletons are found buried under the nave during this restoration work.

1890 The Sheepstor sexton's fee for digging a grave is said to be much too low, so in this year it is increased from 4s to 5s (25p). ◆ Henry Vanstone of Meavy sails for Australia on the ship *Taroba.*

1891 A new organ, built at a cost of £350 by Heles of Saltash, is installed in Chagford Church. ◆ Six passengers spend two nights marooned on the Princetown train, having become engulfed in the drifting snow.

1892 The last broad-gauge train from Penzance to Exeter stops at South Brent (and other southern Dartmoor stations en route) on a week-end in May, before the line is lifted and relaid to standard gauge.

1893 Work begins on the construction of the Burrator Dam.

1894 The Dartmoor Exploration Committee is formed by Burnard, Worth and others. The first site that they explore is the settlement at Grimspound, and a full report of their archaelogical survey appears in the *Transactions of the Devonshire Association.* ◆ The organ at Lustleigh Church is cleaned and repaired for £16. Nearly a century later, in 1980, similar work will cost £2,237.

1895 Wrangaton Golf Club opens. ◆ A Bronze Age flint scraper, now in the Plymouth Museum, is found on Three Barrows. ◆ William and Walter Hill are defendants in a suit brought against them for enclosing Arthur's Hill in Peter Tavy. They lose the case.

1896 Richard Nicholls Worth, the first of two generations of Worths who between them would make such a valuable contribution to Dartmoor exploration and literature, dies and is buried at Shaugh Prior. ◆ Mogridge and Bayldon lease the Hensroost Mine sett from the Duchy for £5 p.a. and 5% dues on ores raised.

1897 A workman named R. Furze unearths a hoard of Roman coins in Okehampton Park. They date from around 320-330 AD.

1898 Burrator Reservoir is officially opened.

1899 Amongst the items sold to Widecombe School for the children's annual treat are 5lb of sweets. The cost? – 2s 1d! (just over 10p).

*****

The Twentieth Century

1900 The official opening of the cottage hospital at Moretonhampstead, built by Viscount Hambledon, the son of W. H. Smith.

1901 Sally Satterly of Jolly Lane Cot dies. She is borne to her final resting place in Widecombe churchyard over the ancient Corpse and Church Way from Hexworthy to Widecombe, the pall-bearers probably resting her bier on the Coffin Stone on Dartmeet Hill en route.

The Coffin Stone on Dartmeet Hill, its surface bearing the initials of some who have rested there on their final journey to Widecombe Church (q.v. 1901).

1902 Cornwood gets its first piped water supply, from a reservoir built on the glebe land.

1903 South Brent parishioners beat their bounds for the first time since 1871.

1904 Proposals for an extension of the old M&SDR route from Moreton to Chagford having been abandoned, the GWR begins operating a bus link between the two towns.

1905 A magnificent organ, the finest to be seen in any Dartmoor church, is installed at Moretonhampstead in a specially constructed loft above a balcony built on the north side of the chancel. Part of the major restoration and enlargement of the church was funded by

W. F. D. Smith, and the church reopens in April after having been closed for some time whilst the work was in progress.

1906 The army, already firmly established at Okehampton since 1875, enhance their claim to a permanent presence on Dartmoor by laying over seven miles of tracks on the Okehampton Range. ◆ Abbot Boniface Natter of Buckfast is drowned in a shipwreck on a voyage to South America.

1907 A permanent tea shelter is built at Fingle Bridge, on the site of the present Anglers' Rest. ◆ The foundation stone is laid for the rebuilding of Buckfast Abbey.

1908 Alexander Hugh Bruce, Baron Balfour of Burleigh, becomes Lord Warden of the Stannaries. ◆ Messrs Willey & Co gain the contract for the supply and maintenance of lamp-posts, lanterns, incandescent burners and mantels, and the lighting and extinguishing of the lights in South Brent from 12 August to 23 March each year. The cost is 45s (£2 25p) per lamp.

1909 The first edition of William Crossing's *Guide to Dartmoor* is published by the *Western Morning News* – at a price of 3s (15p)! ◆ An ancient cross is discovered near Harford Moor Lane, on the old route between South Brent and Plympton, and is subsequently re-erected in the corner of the churchyard where it remains to this day. A report of the find is recorded in the vestry minutes.

1910 The owners of the Prince of Wales Inn at Princetown are the New Passage Brewery Company of Devonport. Their tenant is a J. Budd.

1911 Sir Edwin Lutyens begins building Castle Drogo. It was completed in 1930.

1912 Bishop Trefusis dedicates Yelverton Church to St Paul. The total cost of the newly-built church, begun two years earlier, comes to £5,689, over £1,000 more than the original estimate.

1913 Sydney French leaves Vitifer Mine to work as a road contractor on resurfacing the Two Bridges-Moreton road.

1914 Beatrice Chase's first Dartmoor book, *The Heart of the Moor,* is published. 77,000+ copies are sold. ◆ Mr J. E. D. Moysey of Venton rides a motorcyclette across the moor from South Brent to Princetown, in response to a wager that it could not be done in under 12 hours. The journey takes 4 hours 5 minutes.

1915 The curious-looking building on the Princetown-Two Bridges road known as The Ockery (built in 1809) is demolished. The original barn still stands, on the opposite side of the Blackabrook to the former site of the dwelling, and has been re-roofed in recent years.

1916 The painted wooden board displaying the royal arms of Charles II in Sourton Church is restored by Herbert Read of Exeter.

1917 Corporal Hubert John Green of Buckfastleigh, who joined the 16th Volunteer Battalion Rifle Brigade in early 1915, is killed in Flanders during an attack on Passchendaele Ridge. He is, of course, just one of the many hundreds of Dartmoor men and women who have given their lives for king and country in the two world wars, and in other conflicts around the globe from all periods of history, and the inclusion of Corporal Green's name here is intended to represent them all, and to serve as a testimonial to every single one of them.

1918 An inventory and terrier of Princetown Church records that the prison pays £100 p.a. towards the upkeep of the church. ◆ Throughout the war John Durant of Okehampton had made very frequent visits to the Cranmere Pool area in order to collect sphagnum moss for wounded troops. His entry in the visitor's book for November 18th 1918 records that "The German Fleet has surrendered today". ◆ Ravens from Sourton Quarry are sent to the Tower of London.

1919 The Plymouth Corporation let the unenclosed portions of Yennadown to a Walter Cooper of Plymouth for £4 p.a. A cab operator by trade, the lease permits Cooper to train and excercise his horses on the down.

1920 A war memorial is erected on the south side of the village square at Ugborough at a cost of £200. Tragically, a generation later more names had to be added to it, as, of course, they had to be to parish, town and village memorials throughout the nation.

1921 Charles John Robert H. S. F. Trefusis, Baron Clinton, becomes Lord Warden of the Stannaries. ◆ Edward, Prince of Wales, visits the Cranmere Pool letterbox. His signature is preserved on a page of one of the visitors' books.

1923 An Ugborough Church terrier notes the existence of a "right of way from the eastern gate of the churchyard to the road over the property of the owner of Palk Villa", a right which the owner acknowledges. This ancient way to the eastern side of the graveyard is still open to this day. ◆ William C. Gregor, ex-national hunt jockey, and rider of 647 winners, dies at South Brent.

1924 Ellen Kate Belchar, a postgirl aged 21, is drowned at Cadover Bridge whilst on her postal round. ◆ Advert in the *Western Morning News*: "Postbridge. Furnished Caravan, 3 bunks from 2½ guineas, 30s for 6 months, Bourchier, Woodwater, Exeter", referring to the 'gypsy' caravan first brought to Runnage by Jack Bourchier in 1922, where it remained until it was accidentally destroyed by fire in 1991.

1925 Kingsett Farm, the last working farm in the Newleycombe Valley,

Cadover Bridge, scene of a tragic accident (q.v. 1924).

is finally abandoned to nature and the elements after a documented history spanning six centuries.

1926 A suspension bridge is built at Burrator, on a temporary diversion of the road to Sheepstor whilst the Burrator Dam is being heightened.

1927 Amongst the fictional stories in this year's *Doidge's Annual* are three with a Dartmoor setting – 'The Mystery of Wistman's Wood',

Dartmoor ponies at the ruins of Kingsett Farm (q.v. 1925).

'Mis Tor – A History' and 'Fairies' Hole'.

1928 Lord Hambleden dies, and with him die the Domesday manors of Moretonhampstead and North Bovey, which have been in existence for more than a millennium. In order to meet the staggering death duties, well in excess of £1m, the estates are sold off piecemeal. The new manor house of North Bovey, built only a couple of decades earlier, is purchased by the Great Western Railway for conversion to a golfing hotel. It is today the Manor House Hotel. ◆ William Crossing dies and is buried in Mary Tavy churchyard. The epitaph on his headstone makes no mention of his enormous contribution to Dartmoor literature.

1929 There are just 251 households in Horrabridge which are registered as users of electricity (probably representing only a third of the properties in the village). ◆ Contemporary adverts for the Duchy Hotel, Princetown (now the High Moorland Visitor Centre) proudly proclaim that it has "Electric Light Throughout".

1930 Scenes for Gainsborough Pictures' *The Hound of the Baskervilles* are filmed at the Manor House Hotel, which was chosen as 'Baskerville Hall'. It is a curious circumstance that, although eminently suitable, the building was not, in fact, completed until five years after the publication of Conan Doyle's most famous novel, and so could not have been one of his sources of inspiration for the *Hound* locations.

1931 A grey flint hand axe of the Bronze Age is discovered near Western Whittaburrow. ◆ R. H. Worth publishes a plan of the Upper Merrivale Tin Mill, the site later chosen by the Dartmoor Tinworking Research Group for its archaeological excavations in the 1990s. ◆ A millennium of farming in the Deancombe Valley is brought to a close upon the death of 90-year old Richard Pengelly, last moorman of Combeshead Farm. He is carried to his final resting-place in Sheepstor churchyard by a horse-drawn cart, said to have been the first – and last! – wheeled vehicle ever to have been seen east of Deancombe Farm.

1932 After 25 years of painstaking toil by a group of monks under the direction of Abbot Vonier, the new Buckfast Abbey is finally completed and is consecrated.

1933 William Robartes, Earl of Radnor, becomes Lord Warden of the Stannaries.

1934 The Plymouth Corporation let the grazing rights on Ditsworthy Warren to W. Manning of Yellow Mead for a rent of £15 per quarter.

1935 The 15th and 16th Earls of Devon both die this year, resulting in a crippling bill for death duties amounting to £22,696. The net income generated by the Powderham Estate (which includes the

700 acres of Walreddon in Whitchurch) for the year thus goes into arrears to the tune of £5,471. The estate had been contracting since the 1890s, and another 450 acres are shed to offset the debt.

1936 A fragment of a cross head is reported to have been found on Three Barrows. Another sighting was reported in 1957, but it has not turned up again since.

1937 E. N. Masson Phillips discovers the head of Drywells Cross in a hedge bank. It has since been restored to its rightful place in the wall at the crossroads en route from Jordan to Widecombe.

1938 Following a public outcry the old almshouses in Moretonhampstead are saved from demolition.

1939 A Dartmoor sheep-bell belonging to Mrs Caunter of Dunnabridge is described by Richard H. Worth in the *Transactions of the Devonshire Association.* ◆ Meavy parishioners hold a Dartmoor 'Broom Dance' in the Royal Oak on Christmas Eve, a tradition not reinstituted after the end of the war.

1940 The 59th and 63rd Field Gun Batteries of the Royal Artillery, on manoevres near Chagford, announce that they are going to requisition the gents' conveniences in the town!

1941 Eighty evacuated children from Acton, West London, together with their teachers, arrive in Moretonhampstead.

1942 The Ministry of Supply pays £932 0s 9d to the city of Plymouth for 17.1 acres of standing timber at Burrator.

1943 G. C. Hayter-Hames of Chagford becomes Sheriff of Devon.

1944 The Glen Miller Band plays a concert at RAF Harrowbeer.

1945 RAF Harrowbeer is closed.

1946 The post-war fuel crisis gives a renewed, but very short, lease of life to the Rattlebrook Peat Works, as lorries use the old tramway track to bring down peat turves to serve as a substitute for coal.

1947 Two million sheep are drowned in Britain in the worst floods ever recorded, during the thaw of the winter snows. Many farmers on Dartmoor loose large numbers of livestock.

1948 Charles, later to become Prince of Wales and Duke of Cornwall, is born.

1949 Mrs Douglas-Pennant becomes the new Master of the Dartmoor Foxhounds. ◆ Princess Margaret attends Buckfastleigh Races.

1950 The Rowes of Great Frenchbeare become the new lessees at Teignhead Farm.

1951 Dartmoor becomes a national park.

1952 Electricity is installed in Cornwood Church. ◆ Hawson Cross is re-erected below the Stumpy Oak, Buckfastleigh.

1953 Three years after his death, the executors of Richard Hansford Worth publish *Dartmoor*, a compendium of his papers and other

Hawson Cross and Stumpy Oak (q.v. 1952).

learned articles which for some years the author had intended to publish in book form, an ambition which he was unfortunately not to realise during his lifetime. He is buried at Shaugh Prior alongside the grave of his father. ◆ The Dartmoor Commoners' Association is formed.

1954 Cad Lane, in Ashburton, formerly Back Lane, has its name changed yet again, to Stapleton Lane, after the bishop of that name who had close associations with the town.

1955 Olive Katherine Parr, better known as Beatrice Chase, dies and is buried in Widecombe churchyard. ◆ Thomas Symons dies, aged 89, and is buried at Whitchurch. He had been a bellringer since he was aged 19 and Captain of the Tower for the past 30 years. His position as captain is taken by Harry Mudge (who himself had been a ringer since 1920), a post which he was to hold for 25 years until he died in 1980, aged 76.

1956 The Ebeneezer Bible Christians Chapel in Horrabridge, opened in 1878, closes. ◆ Also closed, in March, is the Princetown railway line from Yelverton.

1957 The building of the Avon Dam, begun in 1954, is completed.

1958 An article in *Devon & Cornwall Notes & Queries* suggests that the Toops of the late-eighteenth and early-nineteenth centuries, members of the well-known Horrabridge firm of stonemasons, carpenters and general builders, were "probably a local musical family"!! – John Toop, founder of the firm, had, in fact, taught the choir at Buckland Monachorum in the 1790s.

1959 The last year of the Buckfastleigh Races and also of passenger services on the Moretonhampstead branch of British Rail.

1960 The first Ten Tors Expedition Challenge is held, which has since become an annual event. ◆ Plans are put forward for RAF Harrowbeer to become the airport for Plymouth. The bill is later defeated in the House of Commons. ◆ Eden Phillpotts, novelist, essayist, poet and playwright, dies at the age of 98: following cremation, his ashes are scattered on Dartmoor.

1961 Frederick Syms, who lived at Huntingdon in the 1950s, and was known to Eric Hemery and others as MooRoaMan, dies at Kingsteignton, aged 86.

1962 The Home Office issues an order for the reinterment of four German airmen killed in an air crash near Burrator in 1941, and buried at Sheepstor in that year. Early the following year (1963) their remains are removed under licence and taken to the German war cemetery at Cannock Chase, Staffs. ◆ The Dartmoor Livestock Protection Society is formed.

1963 Fernworthy Reservoir is frozen to a depth of 18 inches. Most of the roads on central and eastern Dartmoor are impassable for weeks.

1964 The school at Foggintor, at what is now known as Four Winds, is demolished.

1965 Geoffrey Noel Waldegrave, Earl Waldegrave, becomes Lord Warden of the Stannaries. ◆ Michael Heseltine becomes MP for Tavistock.

1966 The Finch Foundry Trust is formed to preserve and restore the edge tool mill at Sticklepath, now the Finch Foundry Museum.

1967 The discovery of an 1840 map of the Parker of Saltram Estates of Shaugh Prior, Cornwood and Plympton St Mary is reported in *Devon & Cornwall Notes & Queries.*

1968 The Dartmoor Rescue Group is formed. ◆ Brent Moor House is blown up by the Royal Marines.

1969 In the face of rising costs and the diminishing quality of reserves, the last surviving hard-rock mine in Devon, Great Rock Mine, near Hennock, closes. ◆ Over a 24-hour period, 5½ inches of rain falls on Princetown. A typical autumn or winter day on high Dartmoor? No – the day in question was at the end of July!

1970 John Bishop's House at Swincombe is featured in the film *The Stallion.* ◆ Granite from Swelltor is transported across the Atlantic in the freighter *Brasilia* – replacement corbels for the old London Bridge, bought by Lake Havasu City, Phoenix, Arizona. New corbels which were not required still lie abandoned beside one of the old railway sidings at Swelltor.

1971 The semi-derelict buildings at Teignhead Farm are demolished.

1972 Work is finally completed on the destruction of another part of what is purportedly a national park – Meldon Reservoir opens.

1973 The last year of operations at Bullycleaves Quarry, which closes the following year.

1974 A mutilated cross found at Burham is re-erected at Yennadon Cross. Recent research has raised questions over whether this was, in fact, the place where the cross originally stood.

1975 Horrabridge is twinned with Tilly. A footbridge built some years later, to provide a safer means of crossing the river (especially for children) just downstream of the ancient road bridge, takes its name from the French village.

1976 Another well-loved Dartmoor landmark disappears when Bawden's Bungalow is demolished.

1977 An ancient wayside cross is discovered at Throwleigh Barton. It has since been re-erected in the churchyard.

1978 Throwleigh is cut off by blizzards in February and runs out of essential supplies. A former inhabitant of the village, George, who had just moved to South Zeal, makes a 3½-mile trek across the snow from the latter village to take a sledge full of provisions to his old home. George, by the way, is a donkey!

1979 A clock is installed in the tower of St Pancras, Widecombe, given by Mrs M. Harris in memory of her husband. It is dedicated on the 341st anniversary of the Great Storm.

1980 The rector of Sampford Spiney reports to the vestry that all records over 100 years old are to be lodged with the County Archives in Exeter, "by law...to preserve them from damp and decay". Four years later an original register from the parish, which had somehow remained in private hands, was sold at auction to a private collector in Bristol!

1981 South Brent Parish Council declare that in future the first 1½ hours of all council meetings will be smoke-free. Smoking will be permitted after 9pm.

1982 Ashburton, twinned with Cleder, France, in 1975, is twinned with Ashburton, New Zealand this year, thereby creating a situation which is by definition not possible (a fact which appears to have escaped the notice of the people who dream up these strange schemes) – how can a 'twin' be one of three?! The two Ashburtons are the only two places in the world which are so named.

1983 Gidleigh Castle is put on the market for £95,000 – 50 years earlier it had been bought for just £700!

1984 The Kelly Mine Preservation Society is formed. Restoration of the site commences the following year, and is still continuing.

1985 Margaretta Mudge dies, aged 82, and is buried at Whitchurch. A small tablet in the church there records that she had been a member of the choir for 71 years. ◆ The first issue of the *Dartmoor Magazine* is published.

1986 Eric Hemery, author of *High Dartmoor* &c, dies and is buried at Meavy. His grave is appropriately bedecked with heather, and bears this simple tribute – "Musician & Dartmoor Author/Like the Cycle of the Waters/We, too, are of Eternity".

1987 The bulldozers move in and flatten the site of the centuries-old Ivybridge Manor Mills (the last buildings, Glanville's Mill, were, in fact, demolished during the previous decade). Where there had once been a grist mill, a malt mill, an edge tool factory, a coal merchants, a grain warehouse, a smithy, a tannery and three houses or cotts at various times during its history, now stands Ivybridge Shopping Centre, the first shops in which opened in 1988. ◆ By contrast, David Bellamy visits Meavy School to award the children with a cheque for £500 for being regional winners in a conservation competition. ◆ Meanwhile, "Houses That Are All Windows" appear in the treetops at Bellever!!!

1988 The Dartmoor Signpost Society is founded, with the expressed aim of placing wooden nameboards on all the tors, and erecting directional signposts to them. The founding date of the society is 1 April!! ◆ The controversial Okehampton bypass, skirting the northern edge of the national park, is opened.

1989 Forest Publishing is established and the following year produces facsimile editions of the Rev H. Hugh Breton's *Beautiful Dartmoor, The Forest of Dartmoor,* and *Spiritual Lessons from Dartmoor Forest.* ◆ Creason Wood, Horndon, is bought by the Woodland Trust.

1990 In the worst gales to hit southern England for many years, huge swathes of forests and woodlands are decimated. On Dartmoor, severe storm damage occurs at Fernworthy, Bellever, Burrator and other places, large stands of pine trees being flattened and thrown around like matchsticks in the hurricane-force winds.

1991 The first issue of *The Dartmoor Newsletter* is published. ◆ An archaeological dig near Sourton Cross unearths 2,000 pieces of Barnstaple pottery ware and other artefacts amongst the remains of a medieval settlement. ◆ The Dartmoor Tinworking Research Group begins its first season of excavation at the Upper Merrivale blowing house.

1992 The Kelly Mine Preservation Society wins the Edward Morshead Trophy for its preservation work. ◆ Arthur Brown retires after 30 years as reeve of Holne Moor.

1993 The discovery of a hitherto unrecorded landscape feature on the fringes of western Dartmoor is widely acclaimed in the popular press and learned journals. However, following extensive research by archaeologists and other interested parties, nothing even remotely resembling it is located on the ground, and so the 'Plymouth/Burrator Corridor' is soon dismissed as being a figment of the imagination of some feeble-minded beaurocrat.

1994 St Michael of the Rock, Brentor, is struck by lightning and the tower severely damaged. ◆ In stark contrast, another event taking place 400,000 million miles away shows how puny this lightning strike is – the titanic explosion caused by the impact of the comet Shoemaker-Levy 9 with the atmosphere of Jupiter creates a scar which is twice the size of the planet Earth (and is recorded in this book as it is certainly <u>the</u> event of the millennium which has been witnessed by man). ◆ Back on 'the third stone from the sun', Mable Mudge, aged 99, retires after having been landlady at the Drewe Arms for 75 years.

1995 The first booklet published by *Dartmoor Press* is released ◆ On the 50th anniversary of VE Day, fires are lit atop Buckland Beacon and many other places on Dartmoor. ◆ A new HQ for the Dartmoor Rescue Group is opened in Tavistock. ◆ The parishioners of

Sourton and Bridestowe beat the bounds of their shared commons.

Certificate issued by the Bridestowe & Sourton Commoners Association (q.v. 1995).

1996 Following public uproar, a massive publicity campaign, and an extremely rowdy meeting at Yelverton village hall, the proposals for the redevelopment of Burrator Reservoir and its environs are shelved.

1997 The nation mourns the death of a princess.

1998 The Dartmoor Society is founded. ◆ The first issue of *Dartmoor – The Country Magazine* is published. ◆ Following a devastating moorland fire the previous year, Trendlebere Down is beginning to regenerate, and rare species of insects and birds are returning to their old habitats.

1999 Ten centuries or so have passed since the Viking raids, and in the opening months of this year there is growing concern about how west Devon will cope with the next 'invasion' – the millions of extra visitors who will descend on the district for the total eclipse! Not surprisingly, the forecasts of impending doom and chaos prove totally unfounded – for, of course, people are quite accustomed to regular periods of darkness which last for many hours, so the fact that it was dark for an extra two minutes one day in August did not affect their reasoning! The anticipated millions also fail to materialise and, although an estimated 45,000 people flock to Plymouth Hoe for the occasion, and large crowds gather at other placers to witness the spectacle, the vagaries of the climate mean that those who stay at home to watch the event on television see more of the sun – or less of it, as the case may be – and then more of it again!

2000 As the first rays of a new dawn break across the frontier heights of Dartmoor, a thousand years have passed since this brief historical overview began. And western Dartmoor is still in a mini state of turmoil. Heightened concerns are being expressed about speed limits and traffic congestion in the national park, erosion of footpaths and bridleways in the most popular spots, the destruction of vernacular buildings and the encroachment of china clay workings and waste dumps. Discussions and investigations are also being held into other issues which are affecting the Dartmoor landscape and the people who live and work in its little hamlets and villages, many of whose ultimate ancestors must have been working the land before the Vikings even set foot on these shores. So, little has changed since that dawn a thousand years ago. Only the costumes and the mode of transport indicate that this is an entirely different era. And the devastation is also being wrought by a new breed of 'invader'. Fortunately, however, there has also been little change in one particular spot on Dartmoor, and Vur Tor still rears its massive granite buttress majestically above the northern wastes, its rocks unmoved by the countless storms which have raged around it for a thousand years. There are no lonely travellers there now, but a large group of people making their annual pilgrimage to the Vur Tor letterbox which nestles in its midst. But, as they scale the rocky heights to survey the scene which surrounds them, their gaze looks out on...nothing! As far as the eye can see there is no sign of human habitation, not even a solitary wall to indicate that man has ever been there, just a vast expanse of untamed wilderness which is still (virtually) untouched by human hand. There is as yet still 'nothing' to be seen. Yet there is much to behold, for those who can 'see', and who are able to appreciate it. As Rowe observed – "the native rudeness and untamed simplicity of these upland solitudes become subjects of the deepest interest to those who find pleasure in contemplating nature in her sterner moods and more austere aspects". And that is at least <u>something</u>! It is, in fact, quite remarkable, and the view from Vur Tor is still to be wondered at, and cherished, in this so-called 'civilised' age. What, I wonder, will have befallen this wild place, the 'last great wilderness in southern England', by the dawn of the next millennium?

*****

List of Subscribers

Brian & Valerie	Brixham, Devon.
Richard	South Brent, Devon.
Mr Terence George Ackland	Beeches, 105 Sandygate Mill, Kingsteignton, Newton Abbot, Devon.
Nan Adams	7 Courtfield, Totnes, Devon.
Evelyn Adamson	Haytor Post Office, Newton Abbot, Devon.
Henrik Ahlm	27 Cromwell Close, London.
Callum & Connell Alexander	Kingsteignton, Devon.
Mr E. Algar & Mrs E. Hebblethwaite	13 Elm Road, Mannamead, Plymouth, Devon.
Mr Jem Allaway	13 Culver Close, Bradninch, Exeter, Devon.
The Rev'd Andrew Allen	
F. D. & B. Allen	
Norman J. Allen	2 Maymar Terrace, Whiterock Road, Wadebridge, Cornwall.
Mr Tom Allen	'St. Winifred', 127 Wembury Road, Elburton, Plymouth, Devon.
William T. E. Amery	Buckfastleigh, Devon.
R. G. Amson	91 Hessary Drive, Roborough, Devon.
Janet & Barry Anderson	28 Long Park, Ashburton, Devon.
Mr J. A. Andrews	73 Abingdon Road, Barming, Maidstone, Kent.
Mr & Mrs R. Andrews	Berescott, Roborough, Devon. (2 copies)
Allan Ashby	8 Roman House, Park Lane East, Reigate, Surrey.
N. F. Ashmore	White Rose Nursery, Callington, Cornwall.
Michael Ashton	Yelverton, Devon.
Hilary Atkinson & Katherine Stone	21 Blundell Drive, Birkdale, Southport, Merseyside.
Dr Michael J. Atwill	Hove-To, 1 Moorings Reach, Brixham, Devon.
Mark Ayers	35 Western Road, Ivybridge, Devon.
L. H. G. Bailey	'Hillingdon', Hennapyn Road, Torquay, Devon.
Mr John Bainbridge	Teignmouth, Devon.
Mr & Mrs M. Banyard	77 Ratcliffe Road, Farnborough, Hants.
Bob Barber	Bray Shop, Cornwall.

Mr N. Barber	25 Spring Grove, Fetcham, Leatherhead, Surrey.
M. J. Barkas	Ashburton, Devon.
Mr & Mrs Peter Barker	Sea Meadow, Higher Sea Lane, Charmouth, Dorset.
R. A. & W. L. Barker	Avery Hill, Kingsteignton, Devon.
Mrs Wendy A. Barker	Kennington, Ashford, Kent.
Fredric Barlow, B.E.M.	22 Northfield Road, Okehampton, Devon.
The Barnes Family	Wormit, Fife.
Maureen Bartle (neé Hamlyn)	Kalgoorlie, Australia.
D. Batehup	Haywards Heath, Sussex.
Mr Jorg Beasley	Yeoford, Devon.
Mrs L. Beckett	Moreton, Wirral, Merseyside.
Mrs S. Beckett	Twickenham, Middx.
Pauline Bedborough	Moorshop, Tavistock, Devon. (2 copies)
Vicki Beer	Eggworthy House, Sampford Spiney, Yelverton, Devon.
Miss C. F. Belam	Ludgate, West Buckfastleigh, Devon.
Rev'd John & Dr Hazel Bell	The Rectory, Kingsnympton, Umberleigh, Devon.
Richard K. Bennett	52 Briar Rd., Hartley, Plymouth, Devon.
Mr Stewart R. Bergman	2 Margaret Road, Ogwell, Newton Abbot, Devon.
Brian & Lorraine Bewsher	Holme Hurst, Old Totnes Road, Buckfastleigh, Devon.
Mr Richard Bilas	3 Chequetts Close, Callington, Cornwall.
Mr C. T. Bishop	11 Meadowpark, Ipplepen, Newton Abbot, Devon.
J. L. & G. M. Bishop	Hartyland, Postbridge, Devon.
R. J. Bishop	18 Brooks Close, Tonbridge, Kent.
Ken Biss	39 Parkhurst Road, Torquay, Devon.
Eric & Heather Blatchford	'The Nest', 7 Erica Drive, Barton, Torquay, Devon.
David R. Blezard	Okehampton, Devon.
Ewart & Margaret Blowey	Mount Tavy, Tavistock, Devon.
Jim Boddy	Shiphay, Devon.
Mrs Kenneth Bolt	27 Plaistow Crescent, St. Budeaux, Plymouth, Devon.
Alan Boon	14 Rock Park, Ashburton, Devon.
Mrs S. Boustead	Newton Abbot, Devon.
Mrs K. Boutland	33 Manstone Lane, Sidmouth, Devon.
Mr I. G. Bowkley	Endsleigh, Sticklepath, Okehampton, Devon.
Michael, Linda & Darren Boxall	5 Woodchurch, The Crescent, Crapstone, Devon.
Mrs Patricia J. Bradbury	59 Barnfield Rd., Paignton, Devon.
Jean Bradshaw	Larwood, 13 Higher Street, Cullompton, Devon.

Mr & Mrs K. Bragg & Master P. Bragg	25 Moor End, Holyport, Maidenhead, Berks.
Mrs D. J. Branton	Higher Penquite Fm., Landrake, Saltash, Cornwall.
Gordon Bray	Burwash, Sussex. (2 copies)
Dave Brewer	Moorfield, Meopham, Kent.
Kath Brewer	Barton, Torquay, Devon.
Brian A. Britten	88 Charfield Drive, Eggbuckand, Plymouth, Devon.
Ray Brooking	267 Crownhill Road, Plymouth, Devon.
Rachel Broomfield	21 Hooe Road, Plymouth, Devon.
Charles & Caroline Brown	Healdsburg, California, U.S.A.
Erica Brown	Park Hill House, Old Mill Road, Chelston, Torquay, Devon.
Dr Bob Bruce	8 Abbotts Park, Cornwood, Ivybridge, Devon. (2 copies)
Valerie Buckingham	Exeter, Devon.
Mr Stuart Bulley	Exminster, Devon.
Chris & Steve Bullock	Laira, Plymouth, Devon.
Simon Bunday	19 Berrys Wood, Bradley Barton, Newton Abbot, Devon.
Hazel M. Burke	The Lodge, 10 Weekaborough Close, Marldon, Devon.
K. J. Burrow	Bucks Cross, Devon.
Dr J. Burston	Tanyards, Rowsells Lane, Totnes, Devon. (2 copies)
Peter Butler	58 Braden Road, Penn, Wolverhampton, West Midlands.
Bob & Jan Callicott	Yate, Bristol.
L. R. Callow	54 Ferndale Rd., Teignmouth, Devon.
Richard & Sue Callow	The Rock Inn, Yelverton, Devon. (2 copies)
Dennis Camp	Plymouth, Devon.
Denis Carnaby	Woodfield Lodge, Torwood Gardens Road, Torquay, Devon.
Joan Carpenter	Westmorland House, 98 Avenue Road, Torquay, Devon.
Aileen Carrett	Liverton, Newton Abbot, Devon.
Mr Barry John Carter	Headington Quarry, Oxford.
Katherine Carter	Catchers Creek, Coombe Road, Shaldon, Devon.
Kristian Carter	Warminster, Wilts.
Patrick Cashell, Esq.	Brook Cottage, Peter Tavy, Tavistock, Devon.
Nicholas Casley	Peverell, Plymouth, Devon.
Dr Michael P. L. Caton	Wylde House Cottage, Gloucester Rd., Ledbury, Herefordshire.
Eva & Mike Chandler	'Stoneleigh', 5 Weech Close, Dawlish, Devon.

B. F. & D. R. Chapman	16 Bowhays Walk, Eggbuckland, Plymouth, Devon.
Hazel Chapman	Park Hill House, Old Mill Road, Chelston, Torquay, Devon.
B. Chapple	9 Sarum Close, Hartley Vale, Plymouth, Devon.
J. E. M. Childs	Albrae, Collaven, Sourton, Okehampton, Devon. (2 copies)
Paul Chown	Bovey Tracey, Devon.
Mr Leslie Clack	Bradninch, Exeter, Devon.
Mrs H. P. Clark	7 Gloucester Road, Stratton, Cirencester, Glos. (2 copies)
Rod Clark	22a Haldon Ave., Teignmouth, Devon.
Ruth Clark	Nottingham.
Mr Arthur Clarke	57 St. Leonards Road, Newton Abbot, Devon.
Pat Clatworthy	1 Dryfield, Exminster, Exeter, Devon.
Ms Jeanne Clutten	19 Dean Street, Langley Mill, Nottingham.
Mr D. W. Cole	Paignton, Devon.
M. J. Colegate	3 Higher Hendham Barns, Woodleigh, Kingsbridge, Devon.
John Coley	Restharrow, Kennerleigh, Crediton, Devon.
Miss Angela Collins	Higher Mill, Peter Tavy, Tavistock, Devon.
Mr M. R. Collins	8 Vicarage Close, Menheniot, Cornwall.
George Colton	Cornwood, Ivybridge, Devon.
Barry Coombes	Weirfield, 49 Southey Lane, Kingskerswell, Devon.
Mr Reg Coombes B.E.M.	Summerhayes, 31 Essa Road, Saltash, Cornwall.
Peter Cooper	Trewinnick Cottage, St. Ervan, Wadebridge, Cornwall.
Mrs Joan Copper	76 Arthur Street, West Bromwich, West Midlands.
Judith Cosford	Moor Park, Chagford, Devon.
P. D. Couch	Plymdene, Heavitree, Exeter, Devon.
Alan Courts	Hamel Down, Harrowbeer Lane, Yelverton, Devon.
P. S. Cousins	1 Godre'r Gaer, Llwyngwril, Gwynedd.
Renée Cranch	Oak House, South Brent, Devon.
John Cranfield	Dartmouth, Devon.
Crawfords Crackers	3 Schofields Way, Bloxham, Banbury, Oxford.
Maurice W. Criddle	Teignmouth, Devon.
John & Elaine Cull	12 St. Georges School Court, Fordington, Dorchester, Dorset.
Mr George Dafter	52 Upland Drive, Plymouth, Devon.
Mr W. F. Daggett	3 Barn Close, Littlehampton, West Sussex.
Ann Darlington	Merriott, Somerset.

Dartmoor National Park Authority

Mr K. C. Davey	Plympton, Devon.
Michael G. Davies	Summerleas, Crapstone Rd., Yelverton, Devon. (2 copies)
Mr & Mrs David Davis	23 Cross Street, Moretonhampstead, Devon.
Keith Dawes	Victoria Villa, Victoria Terrace, Clifton, Bristol.
Pat Day	Boscastle, Cornwall.
Frances Daysh	14 Brooklands, Exeter Road, Chudleigh, Devon.
Owen Deane	9 Becket Road, Bovey Tracey, Devon.
Richard Denby	Clifton, Bristol.
Mr M. Dennison	12 Combley Drive, Thornbury, Plymouth, Devon.
G. E. Diggines	4 Haddon Court, Cecil Road, Paignton, Devon.
Mr & Mrs Anthony W. Dodge	Polonaise, 39 Kyl Cober Parc, Stoke Climsland, Callington, Cornwall.
Ian W. Doidge	Fullamoor, Whitchurch, Tavistock, Devon.
G. J. D. Dollard	Delamore, East Rooke, Cornwood, Ivybridge, Devon.
Mr B. P. Domoney	277 Oborne Road, Sherborne, Dorset.
Mr Philip Downs	Thalassa, 26 Highwold, Chipstead, Surrey.
Suzy & Jon Drake	38 Fawcett Road, Stevenage, Herts.
Mr David Alexander Duffield	3 Highertown, Horrabridge, Nr. Yelverton, Devon.
Shelagh Duffy	Belleair, Lower Woodside Rd., Wootton Bridge, Ryde, Isle of Wight.
Mr C. D. Dulling	1 Ilton Way, Kingsbridge, Devon.
Mr C. H. E. Dunstan	69 Church Street, Kingsbridge, Devon.
Dr Linda Durman	Wrescombe Court, Yealmpton, Plymouth, Devon.
Mrs D. W. Durnford	Oldbury-on-Severn, Glos.
Mr Paul Dutton	Patcham, Brighton, East Sussex.
Mr W. J. Edmunds	Gribblesdown, South Brent, Devon.
Jeff Edwards	114 St. Peters Rd., Brake Farm, Plymouth, Devon.
Dr Steve Edwards & Debbie Young	Penbre, Sir Gaerfyrddin, Cymru.
Richard Elliott	20 Mitchell Road, St. Austell, Cornwall.
Mr James Evans	103 Butt Park Road, Honicknowle, Plymouth, Devon.
Ray Evans	Bournemouth, Dorset.
Steve Fanstone	Staple Close, Plymouth, Devon.
Elizabeth Farleigh	Plymouth, Devon.
Howard Fay	Maidwell, Northants.
William Fell	Higher Lake House, Woodland, Ashburton, Devon.

Miss M. Fenton	Edgcumbe Cottage, Milton Abbot, Tavistock, Devon.
Mr Richard Field	'Tooleys', Horsham Lane, Tamerton Foliot, Plymouth, Devon.
Michael Fillery	13 Hazel Avenue, Maidstone, Kent.
Mrs G. C. Findeisen	Little Meadow, Belstone, Okehampton, Devon.
Mrs F. M. Fisher	Touchstone Cottage, Sandy Park, Chagford, Devon.
Ted Fitch	2 Park Road, Dartington, Totnes, Devon.
Sylvia Forrow	Dawlish, Devon.
Pam & Bill Foster	Tavistock, Devon.
Val & Ray Foster	26 Treburley Close, Treburley, Launceston, Cornwall.
Elizabeth Francis	Dartmouth, Devon.
Mr L. W. Freeman	1 Abbotsfield Close, Tavistock, Devon.
P. A. French	Kelly Bray, Cornwall.
Linda Freshwater	14 Ashtree Close, Woolwell, Plymouth, Devon.
Jason Frost	'Sittaford', Burroughes Avenue, Yeovil, Somerset.
John Gaffney	55 Winston Road, Exmouth, Devon.
Dr Christopher Gardner-Thorpe	The Coach House, 1a College Road, Exeter, Devon.
Alan & Gill Garland	90 Burley Grove, Downend, Bristol.
Mrs Tricia Gerrish	Exmouth, Devon.
M. C. Gilbert	29 Dunstone Road, Plymouth, Devon.
Gerald & Joan Gill	2 Davis Court, Highweek Road, Newton Abbot, Devon.
Mr N. S. Gilliam	8 Trelawne Cottage Gardens, Trelawne, Looe, Cornwall.
David & Rosemary Glanville	3 Lashbrook, Talaton, Exeter, Devon.
Glidden & The Ghost	'Rugglestone', 2 Station Rd., St. Newlyn East, Nr. Newquay, Cornwall.
C. V. & Mrs J. M. Godwin	Olchard House, Olchard, Sandygate, Newton Abbot, Devon.
M. H. Goodall	58 Rymond Road, Birmingham.
Dave & Jenny Goodman	South Molton, Devon.
Mrs J. R. Gough	West Yard, North Bovey, Devon.
Crispian & Elizabeth Graves	Windtor Cottage, Dunstone, Widecombe-in-the-Moor, Devon. (2 copies)
Mrs D. & Mr P. Gray	30 The Village, Bickleigh, Plymouth, Devon.
Mr Neal Gray	23 Badgers Way, Bovey Tracey, Devon.
Allen Greenfield	Tavistock, Devon.
Dr T. & Mrs E. Greeves	39 Bannawell St., Tavistock, Devon.
Mr & Mrs D. Grigg	Plympton, Plymouth, Devon.
Mr & Mrs S. Grigg	Plymstock, Plymouth, Devon.

Gavin Grimsey	Bovey Tracey, Devon.
Stella Grimsey	Overton, Hants.
Mr & Mrs R. Grose	160 Creakavose Park, St. Stephen, St. Austell, Cornwall.
Barbara Groves	Penryn, Cornwall.
Mr & Mrs A. Gurney	5 Tyberton Place, Coley Park, Reading, Berks.
Mrs Diana B. Hall-Say	St. Stephens House, 42 St. Stephens Hill, Launceston, Cornwall.
Alan Halpin	49 Mountpleasant Ave., Exmouth, Devon.
Peter R. Hamilton-Leggett, BSc.	Walkhampton, Devon.
Mr N. Handley	Plymouth, Devon.
Mr Glenn M. Hannigan	'Woodmead', Tavistock, Devon.
Dr & Mrs P. Harbottle	Whitchurch Road, Tavistock, Devon.
Pauline & Robert Hardy	89 Angotts Mead, Stevenage, Herts.
Bruce & Diana Harris	'Cobblers Cottage', The Square, Ipplepen, Devon.
C. D. & M. E. Harris	6 Parklands, Okehampton, Devon.
Dean Harris	10 Barley Market Street, Tavistock, Devon.
Mr G. Harris	Blue Horizon, Nutbush Lane, Chelston, Torquay, Devon.
Mr & Mrs L. J. Harris	Torquay, Devon.
Mrs S. Harris	Paignton, Devon.
Wendy & David Harris	Ivybridge, Devon.
Mr V. Hart	14 Ashford Close, Plymouth, Devon.
William Hart	Lower Knowle, Lustleigh, Devon.
Mervyn P. Harvey	Barnwell House, Brixton, Plymouth, Devon.
David J. Hawkings	Endale, Enborne Row, Newbury, Berks.
Mrs Jean Pamela Hawkins	4 Court Close, Bitterne, Southampton, Hants.
Mr Michael Hayes	Knightstone, Crapstone Road, Yelverton, Devon.
Mr & Mrs R. A. Hayes	The Shieling, Shaugh Prior, Devon.
Craig (Basil) Hayley	98 Clifford Bridge Road, Coventry, West Midlands.
Julia Hayllor	Blackler Barton Farm, Landscove, Ashburton, Devon.
John Hayward	Mallocks, Tipton St. John, Devon.
P. D. Head	Shute House, Denbury, Newton Abbot, Devon.
Mr P. W. J. Heale	The Spinney, 6 Mayflower Avenue, Newton Abbot, Devon.
Mike Hedges	Clanfield, Hants.
Miss O. Hedley-Smith MBE A.C.I.I.	7 Rainbow Court, Queensway, Torquay, Devon.
Pauline Hemery	Whitefriars, Clearbrook, Devon.
Mr M. S. Herbert	Rose Cottage, North Whilborough, Newton Abbot, Devon.

Matthew & Hannah Hewson	24 De Tracey Park, Bovey Tracey, Devon.
A. J. L. Hill	Wood Lane Cottage, Morchard Bishop, Devon.
David & Hazel Hill	Kington, Herefordshire.
Robert Hill	Wokingham, Berks.
A. R. Hiscox	20 Mannings Meadow, Bovey Tracey, Devon.
G. T. Q. Hoare F.I.M.A., C. MATH.	3 Russett Hill, Chalfont St. Peter, Bucks.
Donald Hobbs	20 Swallowfields, Totnes, Devon.
Mr Peter Hodgkinson	Fazeley, Tamworth, Staffs.
Dr Rod Holcombe	Ashleigh Road, Kingsbridge, Devon.
David Holland	5 Wheatfield Lea, Cranbrook, Kent.
Mr David E. Hooper	Gara, Burrator Rd., Dousland, Devon.
Leslie Hooper	44 Stephenson Drive, East Grinstead, Sussex.
J. M. Hornsby	45 Salisbury Road, Banstead, Surrey.
Patricia Horrell	43 Reddington Road, Higher Compton, Plymouth, Devon.
Bob Howard	The Old Stables, Beggearnhuish, Somerset.
Mr J. K. Howard	Colebrook, Plympton, Plymouth, Devon.
Gloria & Jack Howe	Bristol.
Mrs Anne Howse	7 Wolborough Gardens, Newton Abbot, Devon.
Mr J. R. D. Howse	'Newhaven', South Furzeham Road, Brixham, Devon.
Elizabeth Hubbard	55 Salcombe Rd., Plymouth, Devon.
Mr L. W. Hudson	ex-Newton College boy 1920 – 24.
Gordon e. Hughes DSO, DFC, AEA	Ivy Cottage, Townwood, Poundsgate, Newton Abbot, Devon.
Jennifer Hulbert	2 Danum Drive, Plympton, Plymouth, Devon.
Christopher P. Humphries	Launceston, Cornwall.
Andrew Hunt	23 Westbury Lane, Coombe Dingle, Bristol.
Susan Isaacs	Exeter, Devon.
Ken Isham	St. Austell, Cornwall.
Peter Jackman	2 Mill Cottages, Peter Tavy, Tavistock, Devon.
Annette & Derrick Jefferies	Saul, Gloucester.
Mr P. J. Jeffs	Sandhill Lodge, Sandhill, Gunnislake, Cornwall.
Stephen Jenkins	Dunsford, Devon.
Mr J. Loveys Jervoise, DL	Rowden Manor, Sampford Courtenay, Devon.
Melanie Johns	Crewkerne, Somerset.
Glyn Johnson	Stratford-upon-Avon, Warwickshire.
Michael A. Johnson	Rumleigh Gardens, Bere Alston, Devon.
Sandra & David Johnson	Chelston, Torquay, Devon.
Miss Brenda Jordan	94 White Post Field, Sawbridgeworth, Herts.
Ron Joy	61 Grenville Drive, Tavistock, Devon.
A & B K – G	71 Gloucester Road, Exwick, Exeter, Devon.
Mr & Mrs P. Kay	Abbey Meads, Swindon, Wilts.

Tom Keen	Newton Abbot, Devon.
Chris Kelland	12 Northumberland Place, Teignmouth, Devon.
Concetta M. Kelling	Park View, Bowring Mead, Moretonhampstead, Devon.
Mr & Mrs Rodney Kettel	North Bovey, Devon.
The Kidner Family	Beckhams, Manaton, Devon. (3 copies)
Colin C. Kilvington	Stoke, Plymouth, Devon.
Ken Kirby	Christow, Devon.
Major R. F. Kitchin	Withill Farm, Walkhampton, Devon.
Mr Percy Knight	40 Dunclair Park, Laira, Plymouth, Devon.
Mr R. G. R. Ladd	Roborough, Plymouth, Devon.
David J. Lambert	5 Abney Crescent, Roborough, Plymouth, Devon.
Wendy Lamble	Totnes, Devon.
Mr P. Lane	30 Penrith Gardens, Estover, Plymouth, Devon.
Mike & Karen Lang	Woodstock, Liverton, Devon.
Rachel Lang	Woodstock, Liverton, Devon.
Lesley A. Le Toler	Stoke, Plymouth, Devon. (2 copies)
D. J. Lee	11 Homer Rise, Elburton, Plymouth, Devon.
David C. Lee	Widgery, Exeter Road, Exmouth, Devon.
J. Lee	Tavistock, Devon.
J. E. Lee	15 Landhayes Rd., Redhills, Exeter, Devon.
Marjorie Lee	11 Sutton Bassett, Market Harborough, Leics.
Ron Leighton	Sidmouth, Devon.
Dr M. Lekis	17 Heathfield Close, Bovey Tracey, Devon.
Ian Leonard	32 Grimspound Close, Leigham, Plymouth, Devon.
Robin H. Limmer	Mill House, Broome, Norfolk.
John Lissenden	26 Frobisher Drive, Saltash, Cornwall.
Mr Edwin Lovegrove	Uckfield, East Sussex. (Formerly of Brixton, Devon)
Barry & Patricia Luckraft	7 Falkland Way, Teignmouth, Devon.
Dr E. Lunt	43 Keyham Lane, Humberstone, Leicester.
Mr Philip W. Luscombe	50 North Down Crescent, Plymouth, Devon.
Louise & Patrick Lyons	Yelverton, Devon.
Rachel McAdam	The Bartons, West Street, Malmesbury, Wilts.
Jim McBeth	75 Moorview, Keyham, Plymouth, Devon.
M. P. McElheron	41 Southey Lane, Kingskerswell, Devon.
Chris McIntosh	Shanklin, Isle of Wight.
Dr Angus McKay	Sun Cottage, Perranwell Stn., Truro, Cornwall.
Mr Patrick Maher	Ottery St. Mary, Devon.
John & Shirley Mann	42 Moorland Road, Plympton, Plymouth, Devon.
Mrs G. Manton	25 West Street, Ashburton, Devon.
D. M. B. Marquis	Newbarn Cottage, Newbarn Lane, Westerham Hill, Kent.

D. B. Marsh	Mount Lodge, 2 The Mount, New Street, Chagford, Devon.
David & Pauline Marshall	Southway, Plymouth, Devon.
Nick Martin	8 Swallowcliffe Gardens, Yeovil, Somerset.
Robert Martin	Newton Abbot, Devon.
Helena Mathew	Torquay, Devon.
K. H. & M. Mauermann	Essen, Germany.
C. G. & P. D. May	91 Davies Avenue, Paignton, Devon.
Tristan E. H. May	Chicks, Trusham, Teign Valley, Devon.
Mr J. Maynard	31 Merafield Drive, Plympton, Plymouth, Devon.
Brian Mead	Fardel, Cornwood, Devon.
Christopher John Menlove-Platt	26 Holtwood Road, Glenholt, Plymouth, Devon.
Pam & Alan Meridew	69 Brakefields, South Brent, Devon.
Dr R. Ll. Meyrick	Boulters Tor, Peter Tavy, Devon.
Lt. Col. & Mrs R. A. Middleton	Fair Winds, Southella Road, Yelverton, Devon.
Keith & Alison Miller	York.
Rick Miller	Pinhoe, Exeter, Devon.
Mr Bernie Millington	Firleigh Rd., Kingsteignton, Devon.
Dr A. F. Milward	1 Fulford Cottages, Crockernwell, Exeter, Devon.
Alan & Joan Minter	52 Follaton, Plymouth Road, Totnes, Devon.
Mrs Doreen Mole	Plymouth, Devon.
Mr Jonathan Mole	34 Bennett Place, Ilmington, Shipston-on-Stour, Warwickshire.
Chris Monks	51 Vicarage Rd., Whitehall, Bristol.
Roy Montgomery	Waterlooville, Hants.
Marjorie Moore	Hawson Court, Buckfastleigh, Devon.
Sylvia & Tony Moore	25 Sanderspool Cross, South Brent, Devon.
Y. M. & J. P. Moore	113 Morton Tce., Gainsborough, Lincs.
Mr D. K. Moorse	Fourwinds, Old Roman Bank, Terrington St. Clement, Norfolk.
Helen & Quentin Morgan Edwards	Glebe House, Sampford Courtenay, Devon.
Mrs R. Morley (Allen)	4 Beal Farm Mews, Chudleigh Knighton, Devon. (2 copies)
Mary Myers	Dorchester, Dorset.
Kenneth C. Naylor	3 Trevenn Drive, Kingskerswell, Newton Abbot, Devon.
Bob Noakes	
Janet Nobbs	Tweenaways, Marley, South Brent, Devon. (2 copies)
John Northam F.C.C.A.	Heatherton Grange Hotel, Bradford on Tone, Taunton, Somerset.
Benedetta Novigno	Viale G. Milton 27, 5012Q Firenze, Italia.

Mr P. O' Doherty	Wigginton, Banbury, Oxon.
Mr & Mrs J. O'Neill	Tangle Trees, 32 Warbilington Road, Emsworth, Hants.
Dr. John Ogle	Clearbrook, Devon.
Mr T. L. Orchard	Windyridge, Midella Road, Yelverton, Devon.
Mary Osborn	Yelverton, Devon.
M. J. Osborne	Westbury, Wilts.
Mr Roger Osborne	60a Connaught Avenue, Mutley, Plymouth, Devon.
Miss B. J. Ostler	21 Church St., Modbury, Devon.
Mrs Julie Owen	Inuvik, Shaugh Prior, Plymouth, Devon.
Andy Pain	26 Warecross Gardens, Kingsteignton, Newton Abbot, Devon.
J. & B. Palarm	43 Springfield Park, Mylor Bridge, Cornwall.
Yvonne & Richard Palfrey	Ottery St. Mary, Devon.
Mr F. E. Palk	205 Holcombe Road, Greenmount, Bury, Lancs.
Mr & Mrs B. Palmer	10a Bishopstoke Rd., Eastleigh, Hants.
Ossie & Janet Palmer	24 St David's Road, Tavistock, Devon.
Barbara Papworth	31 Sunnymead Road, Roehampton, London.
Len & Sharon Paramore (Torpoint Trekkers)	Torpoint, Cornwall.
Mrs T. Parnall	Plymouth, Devon.
Dr. Geoffrey Parnell	Maldon, Essex.
J. G. Parnell	Strettel House, Bradley Road, Bovey Tracey, Devon.
Andrew Passmore	Exeter, Devon.
Mike & Jane Passmore	Exeter, Devon.
Roger & Stephanie Paul	Denbury, Devon.
Mrs Annette Pearce	26 Pinn Hill, Pinhoe, Exeter, Devon.
Mrs M. D. Pearce	5 Colmer Road, Yeovil, Somerset.
Roy Pearce	Willand, Cullompton, Devon.
John Pearse	26 Lynwood Grove, Orpington, Kent.
Mrs Margaret Pearse	Tradewinds, Retreat Drive, Topsham, Exeter, Devon.
Pebbles & Co.	4 Big Lane, Lambourn, Berks.
Rosemary Pegrum	36 Hillcrest Road, Loughton, Essex.
B. J. Pengelly	9 Tregarland Close, Coads Green, Launceston, Cornwall.
Kenneth Pepperell	
Linda Perkin	16 Cross Park, Brixton, Plymouth, Devon.
Mr & Mrs R. M. Perry	4 Ainslie Terrace, Camel's Head, Plymouth, Devon.
Dr & Mrs R. J. Pethybridge	64 Fort Road, Alverstoke, Gosport, Hants.
Mr Roy Pettitt	9 South Lawns, Bridport, Dorset.
Mrs Sarah Pettitt	'Barrow', Crossways Road, Grayshott, Hindhead, Surrey.

B. Philips	20 St. Peters Close, Bovey Tracey, Devon.
Mrs L. J. Phillips	8 Grebe Close, Chickerell, Weymouth, Dorset.
Claude Pike	Marwood, Heathercombe, Manaton, Devon.
Jonathan Pike	4 Arbutus Drive, Coombe Dingle, Bristol.
Tony Pink	Abbots Langley, Herts.
Mr M. J. Piper	'Firswood', Manor Drive, Kingskerswell, Newton Abbot, Devon.
Mr M. & Mrs D. M. Plush	
Plymouth City Council	Civic Centre, Plymouth, Devon.
Alan J. Potter	7 Kings Green Avenue, Kings Norton, Birmingham.
Keith Potter	5 Longacre, Harrowbarrow, Callington, Cornwall.
K. A. Pratt	
Brian W. Pugh	20 Clare Road, Lewes, Sussex.
June & Desmond Puttick	Eastbourne, Sussex.
Lesley Pymm & Michael Tracy	Birmingham.
Louise Querner	Adolfstorgasse 2.B., A 1130 Vienna, Austria.
Bill Ransom	Ilsington, Devon.
Mrs Pat Read	8 Armstrong Avenue, Pennsylvania, Exeter, Devon.
Mrs Ann Reed	60 Layfield Road, Hendon, London.
Mr David R. Rees	7 Grosvenor Close, Torquay, Devon.
Mr & Mrs W. A. Reeves	30 Spencer Road, Paignton, Devon.
Alistair Graham Reid	1 Haldon Close, Buckland Estate, Newton Abbot, Devon.
Paul Rendell	The Coach House, Okehampton, Devon.
Mr Matthew Rendle	1 Calthorpe Road, Exeter, Devon.
Nigel W. Rendle	Ivy Cottage, Buckland Monachorum, Yelverton, Devon.
The Restell Family	Sandhurst, Berks.
Ken Rickard	Lydford, Devon.
Mrs C. A. Ridgeon	Lipson, Plymouth, Devon.
R. A. Roach	19 Overton Gardens, Mannamead, Plymouth, Devon.
Miss Janet Robb	393 Topsham Road, Exeter, Devon.
M. C. Robbins	9 Windsor Road, Southport, Merseyside.
Mrs Pat Roberts	Melfort, The Avenue, Chobham, Surrey.
Ru Roberts	Village Farm, Holne, Devon.
Jean Robertson	Loders, Bridport, Dorset. (2 copies)
Syd & Diane Robins	34 Trelawney Road, St. Austell, Cornwall.
Hugh Robinson	Gunnislake, Cornwall.
Dean Rodgers	3 Branson Park, Tavistock, Devon.
Brian Rodwell	Chudleigh, Devon.
Mr John Roles	37 Manor Farm Rd., Tredington, Shipston-on-Stour, Warwickshire.

Colin & Joan Rolfe	Plymouth, Devon.
Mr & Mrs M. Rolfe	Lower Dimson, Gunnislake, Cornwall.
P. A. Romig	22 Park Avenue, Brixham, Devon.
Peter E. Rose	Purley, Surrey.
John W. Rundle	3 King's Court, 102 King Street, Plymouth, Devon.
Mr & Mrs L. D. Sampson	Okehampton, Devon.
Mrs Jenny Sanders	Tavistock, Devon.
Dr Peter Sanders	Park House, Plymtree, Cullompton, Devon.
Tim Sandles	Denbury, Devon.
Peter Saunders	Ringwood, Hants.
Mr R. H. Seaman	68 Rolvenden Road, Wainscott, Rochester, Kent.
Joyce M. Searle	Plymouth, Devon. (4 copies)
Lorna G. Seidel	
Mrs Maureen Selley	Windyridge, Plymouth Road, Horrabridge, Yelverton, Devon.
Sir David Serpell	Dartmouth, Devon. (2 copies)
Mrs Joanne Shaw	7 West Farndon, Northants.
Cecilia Shepherd	Maiden Newton, Dorset.
Sylvia Shepherd	Woodfield Lodge, Torwood Gardens Road, Torquay, Devon.
Mr Anthony Sherwood	46 Southfield Ave., Paignton, Devon.
S. M. Shirley	Aylestone, Leics.
Mr Michael Alan Shorey	3 Swallow Close, Warminster, Wilts.
Miss Celia M. Short	27 Congreve Road, Worthing, West Sussex.
Mr David B. Short	20 Groombridge Way, Horsham, West Sussex.
Chris & Ronnie Sidwell	9a Reed Vale, Teignmouth, Devon.
Richard Silverlock F.R.I.C.S.	Sungarth, St. Austell, Cornwall.
Christopher G. W. Simmons	Hayes, Bromley, Kent.
Mr Robin W. Skinner	59 Goldsmith Road, Worthing, West Sussex.
M. C. Skipwith	Aish Cross House, Aish, Stoke Gabriel, Totnes, Devon.
Roger & Aileen Smaldon	46 Briar Road, Hartley, Plymouth, Devon.
Jim Smale	73 Colt Stead, New Ash Green, Longfield, Kent.
Arthur Smith	Teignmouth, Devon.
Brenda Smith	81 Leighton Road, Weston, Bath, Somerset.
Geoff & Karen Smith	9 Latimer Close, Plympton, Plymouth, Devon.
Miss Hazel V. Smith	'Ash Lea', Widdicombe Drive, Ivybridge, Devon.
Mr Jeremy Smith	Stonehouse, Plymouth, Devon.
John E. Smith	Turnchapel, Plymouth, Devon.
Kate Smith	
Mr & Mrs M. Smith	(2 copies)
Mrs Marguerite C. Smith	64 Longlands Drive, Heybrook Bay, Plymouth, Devon.

Michael B. Smith	30 Moorland View, Newton Abbot, Devon.
Mr Richard Smith	St. Cleer, Cornwall.
Sheila Smith	Nottingham.
Mrs Sue Smith	Halwell, Totnes, Devon.
Mr Wayne Smith	Blackwater, Camberley, Surrey.
Jon Southgate	4 Monmouth Gardens, Plymouth, Devon.
Mrs Maureen Sowerby	
Mr R. G. Spear	
Mrs Gladys Spreadbury	63 Kirby Rd., Portsmouth, Hants.
Mr & Mrs H. J. Stanlake	Saltash, Cornwall.
Jason Steen	9 Acacia Place, London.
Xanthe Steen	9 Acacia Place, London.
Arthur Stephens	15 Mostyn Ave., Lipson, Plymouth, Devon.
Mrs Paula Stephens	21 Ashfield Close, Exmouth, Devon.
The Rev'd S. J. Stephens	Oldbury, West Midlands.
Mr & Mrs R. Stevens	Sadlers Way, Hertford.
Mike Steward	Langford, Sampford Courtenay, Okehampton, Devon. (2 copies)
John Stickland	Shady Coombe, Hoo Meavy, Yelverton, Devon.
Miss J. M. Stivey	Plymouth, Devon.
The Family Stones	'Sunnyside', Princetown, Dartmoor, Devon. (2 copies)
Reverend A. J. Stott	Ivybridge, Devon.
Daniel J. Stowers LLB (Hons)	Ivy Bank, Taddington, Derbyshire.
Chief Supt. John E. Stowers	Wayland Cottage, Tedburn St. Mary, Devon.
Mr B. C. & Mrs W. A. Sugg	Ashbourne, Derbyshire.
Mr R. N. & Mrs J. S. Sutton	16 Bluebell Close, Highcliffe, Christchurch, Dorset.
Brian Maurice Sweet	6 Gilbert Close, St. Stephen, St. Austell, Cornwall.
Donald Symons	1 Dawney Drive, Four Oaks, Sutton Coldfield, West Midlands.
Sylvia Tancock	Paignton, Devon.
Anthony P. Tapp	Kelly Bray, Cornwall.
Mr & Mrs R. J. Taylor	Church Farm, Egerton, Ashford, Kent.
Trevor J. Taylor	Lyndhurst, Linden Ave., Odiham, Hook, Hants.
Lt. Col. & Mrs C. H. Teall	Derncleugh, Holcombe, Dawlish, Devon.
Mrs P. Theobald (neé German)	Marston Lodge, Weydown Road, Haslemere, Surrey.
Joyce Thomas	33 Park Lane, Pinhoe, Exeter, Devon.
R. & I. Thompson	'Carrigeen', North Bovey, Devon.
Mr R. C. Thompson	36 Dickson Rd., Eltham, London.
George Thurlow	Ideford, Devon.
Mrs Carole A. Tinkler	96 Chestnut Drive, Brixham, Devon.

Barbara Tooze	10 North Street, Denbury, Newton Abbot, Devon.
Mrs B. A. Tregay	1 Rolle Cottages, Knowle, Budleigh Salterton, Devon.
Pauline E. M. Trenerry	Bishopsteignton, Devon.
Mrs K. M. Trevan	58 Berwick Ave., Crownhill, Plymouth, Devon.
Pat Trout	208 Pine Avenue, Glynswood, Chard, Somerset.
C. J. & S. M. Trudgian	1 Meadow Park, Trewoon, St. Austell, Cornwall.
A. R. Tulley	Wembury, Devon.
Sandra Urban	Torquay, Devon. (2 copies)
Anne Vallings	Green Pastures, College Road, Newton Abbot, Devon.
Tony Van Beveren	6 Broad Walk, Saltash, Cornwall.
Mrs Kate Van der Kiste	Lavandou, Moorland Park, South Brent, Devon.
Mr & Mrs R. A. Vane	16 Revesby Close, Hartsholme, Lincoln.
Sheron Vowden	'The Forge', Middle Rixdale, Luton, Newton Abbot, Devon.
Anne & Michael Wadmore	18 Fern Close, Okehampton, Devon.
Rev'd Philip Wagstaff	Harwich, Essex.
Peta & Alan Wake	Yelverton, Devon.
Mrs M. G. Wakeford	7 Downsview Road, Portslade, Brighton, East Sussex.
Mr & Mrs G. E. Waldron	38 Waycott Walk, Southway, Plymouth, Devon.
Ian Walker	Greystones, Church St., Barrowby, Lincs.
J. Walker	Marlborough Ave., Torquay, Devon.
John & Anne Walker	Courts Close, Holne, Newton Abbot, Devon.
John F. W. Walling	Kingsteignton, Devon.
Don Waring	Rydal, Llanfair Discoed, Chepstow, Mons.
T. M. & J. Warren	
M. E. Watkins	Southwick, Sussex.
Alan Watson	Exeter, Devon.
Sheila & David Watts	Milverton Road, Winchester, Hants.
Mr I. D. Waugh	Torquay, Devon.
E. & M. Webb	12 Alamein Road, Saltash, Cornwall.
David J. B. Weekes	Honicknowle, Plymouth, Devon.
John J. B. Weekes	Westbury Park, Bristol.
Stefan Weishaupt	Bruchhof 18, 32457 Porta Westfalica, Germany.
Mrs I. M. E. Wellington	Wheal Rose, Smithaleigh, Plymouth, Devon.
A. A. & S. G. West	46 Chadwick Road, Eastleigh, Hants.
Miss Sue West	Ashton, Vaughan Rd., Exeter, Devon.

Westcountry Studies Library	Exeter, Devon.
Mr W. J. Westlake	12 Pikes Mead, Okehampton, Devon.
Dr Donald K. White	13 The Coach House, Steartfield Road, Paignton, Devon.
Eddie White	40 Westbridge Cottages, Plymouth Rd., Tavistock, Devon.
H. A. E. White	Oakley, Bolthouse Close, Tavistock, Devon.
Christopher Whittle	Apple Cottages, Bovingdon, Herts.
Mr R. M. Wightman	Newton Abbot, Devon.
Mr T. J. Wightman	Newton Abbot, Devon.
Maywyn Wilkinson	12 Wallaford Rd., Buckfastleigh, Devon.
Brenda Williams	Paignton, Devon.
Claude & Jean Williams	Harwood Cottage, Horrabridge, Devon.
Mr John B. Williams	Gate House, North Bovey, Devon.
Miss Jayne Williamson	12 Foxley Crescent, Newton Abbot, Devon.
Mr Graham L. Willmott	18 Fairview Avenue, Laira, Plymouth, Devon.
Gerald Wills	6 Elm Green, Hemel Hempstead, Herts.
Anne Wilson	Deniliquin, NSW, Australia.
Christine Winter	251 Victoria Road, St. Budeaux, Plymouth, Devon.
Peggy Woodcock	17 Crokers Way, Ipplepen, Newton Abbot, Devon.
Mr M. R. Woolf	165 Witcombe, Yate, Glos.
Anne R. Workman	Hognaston, Derbyshire.
Captain R. S. Wraith, Royal Navy	Tavistock, Devon.
The Rev'd Geoffrey Wrayford	The Vicarage, 7 Paganel Road, Minehead, Somerset.
Mike & Hilary Wreford	Wilton House, 65 Crediton Rd., Okehampton, Devon.
C. B. Wurtzburg	Old Whitstone, Bovey Tracey, Devon.
Susan Wyeth	Eastfield, 20 Blue Waters Drive, Paignton, Devon.
Christopher Wynn	
Mr & Mrs J. Yandle	Haydon Rise, Dancing Lane, Wincanton, Somerset.
Mrs E. K. Young	114 Torquay Rd., Newton Abbot, Devon.

*****